Hands-On Python and Te

A Practical Guide to Deep Learning

Sarful Hassan

Preface

Welcome to **Hands-On Python and TensorFlow: A Practical Guide to Deep Learning**! This book provides a hands-on approach to learning deep learning with Python and TensorFlow. Whether you're a beginner or an experienced developer, this book will guide you through core concepts and practical applications.

Who This Book Is For

This book is for anyone interested in learning deep learning using Python and TensorFlow. A basic knowledge of Python will help, but no prior machine learning experience is necessary.

How This Book Is Organized

The book is divided into chapters that cover TensorFlow fundamentals, model building, optimization, and practical applications like image classification, object detection, and reinforcement learning. Each chapter includes practical examples and exercises.

What Was Left Out

While comprehensive, this book doesn't cover every machine learning technique. Advanced topics and specialized TensorFlow extensions are outside its scope, but we offer resources for further learning.

Code Style

Code examples follow best practices for Python and TensorFlow. All code can be found in the accompanying repository for you to experiment with and modify.

Release Notes

This book uses TensorFlow and Python's latest versions at the time of publication. Future updates may lead to minor changes in the code.

Notes on the First Edition

This first edition provides a solid foundation in deep learning. Future editions will expand on various topics based on feedback and advancements in the field.

MechatronicsLAB Online Learning

For additional learning resources, visit **mechatronicslab.net** for tutorials and interactive exercises.

How to Contact Us

For questions, contact us at:

- Email: mechatronicslab@gmail.com
- Website: mechatronicslab.net

Acknowledgments

Thanks to all who contributed to this book, especially the TensorFlow and Python communities for their ongoing support.

Copyright (MechatronicsLAB)

Disclaimer

This book is for educational purposes only. The author and publisher are not responsible for any errors or outcomes related to using the code and techniques discussed.

Table of Contents

Chapter-1 Introduction to Python and TensorFlow

TensorFlow is one of the most widely used deep learning frameworks, developed by Google Brain. It provides an open-source platform for building, training, and deploying machine learning models. TensorFlow is highly flexible and can run on CPUs, GPUs, and TPUs, making it a preferred choice for researchers and developers.

Why Python?

Python is the dominant programming language for machine learning and deep learning due to its simplicity, readability, and extensive library support. It integrates seamlessly with TensorFlow, making it an ideal choice for AI development.

Key Advantages of Python for TensorFlow

1. **Ease of Use** – Python's syntax is simple and intuitive, making deep learning more accessible.
2. **Rich Ecosystem** – Libraries such as NumPy, Pandas, and Matplotlib complement TensorFlow.
3. **Community Support** – A vast community provides continuous improvements, tutorials, and troubleshooting resources.
4. **Cross-Platform Compatibility** – Python runs on various operating systems, ensuring flexibility in development.
5. **Integration with AI Tools** – Supports tools like Jupyter Notebooks and Google Colab for interactive development.

What is TensorFlow?

TensorFlow is an end-to-end machine learning framework that enables the creation and deployment of deep learning models. It provides a comprehensive ecosystem for building neural networks efficiently.

Key Features of TensorFlow

1. **Computational Graphs** – Uses graph-based execution for optimization and efficiency.
2. **GPU and TPU Acceleration** – Supports parallel computations on multiple devices.
3. **Keras Integration** – Includes Keras as its high-level API for rapid model development.

4. **TensorBoard** – Provides visualization tools for monitoring training performance.
5. **TF Lite and TF.js** – Enables deployment on mobile devices and web applications.

Why Use TensorFlow with Python?

1. **Scalability** – Handles small to large-scale AI applications.
2. **Extensive Pretrained Models** – Offers prebuilt models and transfer learning options.
3. **Production-Ready** – Used in industry for deploying AI-powered solutions.
4. **Optimized Performance** – Leverages hardware acceleration for faster computations.

Applications of Python and TensorFlow

1. **Computer Vision** – Image classification, object detection, and facial recognition.
2. **Natural Language Processing (NLP)** – Sentiment analysis, speech recognition, and chatbot development.
3. **Healthcare** – Disease diagnosis, medical image analysis, and drug discovery.
4. **Finance** – Fraud detection, risk assessment, and algorithmic trading.
5. **Autonomous Systems** – Self-driving cars, robotics, and AI automation.

TensorFlow, combined with Python's simplicity, provides an efficient and powerful platform for deep learning research and applications. Its versatility and scalability make it a go-to framework for AI-driven solutions.

Chapter-2 Installing TensorFlow and Setting Up the Environment

TensorFlow is a widely used deep learning framework that can be installed on various platforms, including Windows, Linux, macOS, and cloud environments. This guide provides step-by-step instructions for setting up TensorFlow efficiently, ensuring compatibility and smooth operation.

Step 1: Verify System Requirements

Before installing TensorFlow, ensure that your system meets the minimum requirements:

- **Operating System** – Windows 10/11, macOS 10.14 or later, or Linux (Ubuntu 18.04 or later)
- **Python Version** – Python 3.7 or later (recommended: Python 3.9 or 3.10)
- **RAM** – At least 8GB of RAM (16GB recommended for large models)
- **Storage** – Minimum of 5GB free space for TensorFlow and dependencies
- **Hardware** – Compatible CPU or NVIDIA GPU (for GPU acceleration)
- **CUDA and cuDNN (for GPU support)** – Compatible NVIDIA GPU with CUDA 11.2+ and cuDNN 8.1+

Step 2: Create a Virtual Environment (Recommended)

Using a virtual environment isolates TensorFlow and its dependencies, preventing conflicts with other installed packages. To create and activate a virtual environment, use the following commands:

For Windows

```
pip install virtualenv
virtualenv tensorflow_env
tensorflow_env\Scripts\activate
```

For Linux/macOS

```
pip install virtualenv
virtualenv tensorflow_env
source tensorflow_env/bin/activate
```

Step 3: Install TensorFlow

Once inside the virtual environment, install TensorFlow using pip:

```
pip install tensorflow
```

For GPU support, install the GPU version:

```
pip install tensorflow-gpu
```

To confirm that TensorFlow is installed correctly, check the installed version:

```
python -c "import tensorflow as tf;
print(tf.__version__)"
```

Step 4: Install Additional Dependencies

To ensure smooth execution, install commonly used libraries:

```
pip install numpy pandas matplotlib seaborn
```

For GPU users, verify CUDA and cuDNN installation:

```
nvidia-smi
```

Installing TensorFlow on Different Platforms

Windows Installation

1. Install Python and update pip:

```
python -m pip install --upgrade pip
```

2. Install TensorFlow using pip inside a virtual environment.
3. Verify installation with the TensorFlow version check.

Linux Installation

1. Update package manager and install Python dependencies:

```
sudo apt update && sudo apt install python3-pip
python3-dev
```

2. Install TensorFlow inside a virtual environment as shown earlier.

macOS Installation

1. Install Python and dependencies via Homebrew:

```
brew install python
```

2. Install TensorFlow via pip inside a virtual environment.

Raspberry Pi Installation

1. Update the system and install Python dependencies:

```
sudo apt update && sudo apt install python3-pip
```

2. Install TensorFlow Lite for optimized performance:

```
pip install tflite-runtime
```

Anaconda Installation

1. Open Anaconda Prompt and create a new environment:

```
conda create -n tensorflow_env python=3.9
conda activate tensorflow_env
```

2. Install TensorFlow using conda:

```
conda install -c conda-forge tensorflow
```

Step 5: Verify TensorFlow Installation

To confirm that TensorFlow is working correctly, run the following command:

```
import tensorflow as tf
print("TensorFlow version:", tf.__version__)
```

If the installation is successful, you should see the installed TensorFlow version printed in the output.

Step 6: Running a Simple TensorFlow Program

To check if TensorFlow is functioning, run a basic computation:

```
x = tf.constant([[1, 2], [3, 4]])
y = tf.constant([[5, 6], [7, 8]])
result = tf.matmul(x, y)
print("Matrix Multiplication Result:", result.numpy())
```

Common Troubleshooting Tips

- **Installation Fails** – Ensure Python and pip are updated:

```
pip install --upgrade pip
```

GPU Not Detected – Check CUDA and cuDNN installation using:

```
nvidia-smi
```

Performance Issues – Optimize execution by enabling mixed precision training:

```
tf.keras.mixed_precision.set_global_policy('mixed_float
16')
```

ModuleNotFoundError – If TensorFlow is not recognized, ensure you are in the correct virtual environment:

```
source tensorflow_env/bin/activate  # Linux/macOS
# Windows: tensorflow_env\Scripts\activate
```

Once installed and verified, TensorFlow is ready for deep learning development, AI experimentation, and model deployment.

Chapter-3 TensorFlow's Architecture and Ecosystem

TensorFlow is a powerful open-source deep learning framework developed by Google Brain. It provides a flexible and efficient architecture for building machine learning models, from simple neural networks to complex multi-node deep learning applications. This section explores TensorFlow's internal architecture and its extensive ecosystem in greater detail to provide a better understanding of its functionalities.

TensorFlow's Core Architecture

TensorFlow is built on a computational graph-based architecture that enables efficient execution of machine learning models across various platforms, optimizing performance for different hardware configurations.

1. Computational Graphs

TensorFlow represents computations as a directed acyclic graph (DAG), where:

- **Nodes** represent mathematical operations (e.g., matrix multiplications, activation functions, gradient updates).
- **Edges** represent tensors (multi-dimensional data arrays) flowing between operations, carrying data and model parameters.

This graph-based structure enables TensorFlow to optimize computations for distributed execution, reducing memory overhead and improving performance across multiple devices.

2. Tensors: The Core Data Structure

Tensors are the fundamental building blocks in TensorFlow, representing multi-dimensional numerical arrays. These tensors serve as the primary means of storing and manipulating data during computation.

Types of Tensors in TensorFlow:

- **Scalar (Rank 0)** – A single numerical value (e.g., 5).
- **Vector (Rank 1)** – A one-dimensional array (e.g., [1, 2, 3]).
- **Matrix (Rank 2)** – A two-dimensional array (e.g., [[1, 2], [3, 4]]).
- **Higher-Dimensional Tensors (Rank 3+)** – Used in deep learning models, such as 3D tensors for images and 4D tensors for video sequences.

3. Execution Modes: Eager Execution vs. Graph Execution

- **Eager Execution** – Runs operations immediately in an imperative manner, making debugging easier and more interactive.
- **Graph Execution** – Converts operations into a computational graph for deferred execution, allowing optimization through static analysis.

Graph execution enables TensorFlow to perform faster computations by leveraging optimizations like operation fusion, lazy evaluation, and parallel execution.

4. Distributed Computing and Parallelism

TensorFlow supports distributed training using **TensorFlow Distributed Strategy** to scale models across multiple GPUs, TPUs, and clusters.

- **Data Parallelism** – The same model runs on multiple devices, each handling a portion of the data.
- **Model Parallelism** – Different parts of a model are distributed across multiple devices, useful for very large architectures.
- **Hybrid Parallelism** – A combination of data and model parallelism for optimized execution.

TensorFlow's Ecosystem

TensorFlow provides a vast ecosystem of tools and extensions to support the entire machine learning lifecycle, from model development to deployment.

1. Keras: High-Level API for Deep Learning

- Integrated into TensorFlow (tf.keras), providing an easy-to-use high-level API for building and training deep learning models.
- Supports Sequential API, Functional API, and subclassing for custom models.

2. TensorBoard: Model Visualization and Debugging

- Allows visualization of loss curves, computational graphs, and performance metrics in an interactive dashboard.
- Used for hyperparameter tuning, debugging, and tracking model progress.

3. TensorFlow Hub: Pretrained Models for Transfer Learning

- A repository of pre-trained machine learning models that can be easily reused for different tasks.
- Includes models for computer vision (ResNet, MobileNet) and NLP

(BERT, GPT).

4. TensorFlow Lite (TF Lite): Mobile and Edge AI

- Optimized version of TensorFlow designed for running deep learning models on mobile devices, IoT devices, and edge computing hardware.
- Supports model quantization, reducing model size and improving inference speed.

5. TensorFlow.js: Machine Learning in the Browser

- Allows running TensorFlow models directly in web browsers using JavaScript.
- Supports training and inference without server-side dependencies, making it ideal for interactive AI applications.

6. TensorFlow Serving: Deploying Models in Production

- A scalable system for serving machine learning models in real-time applications.
- Supports model versioning, A/B testing, and dynamic inference requests.

7. TensorFlow Extended (TFX): End-to-End Machine Learning Pipelines

- A complete framework for managing production machine learning workflows.
- Includes tools for data validation, feature engineering, model training, evaluation, and deployment.

Comparison of TensorFlow with Other Frameworks

Feature	TensorFlow	PyTorch	Keras	MXNet
Graph Execution	✓	✓	✓	✓
Eager Execution	✓	✓	✓	✓
Distributed Training	✓	✓	✗	✓
Mobile Deployment	✓	✗	✗	✗
Web Deployment	✓	✗	✗	✗

Chapter-4 Key Concepts: Tensors, Graphs, and Sessions

TensorFlow is built on three foundational concepts: **tensors**, **computational graphs**, and **sessions**. These elements enable efficient numerical computations and deep learning model execution across different platforms. Understanding these concepts is crucial for effectively using TensorFlow.

Tensors in TensorFlow

Tensors are multi-dimensional arrays that represent data in TensorFlow. They are the fundamental building blocks for all operations in a computational graph.

Types of Tensors

- **Scalars (Rank 0)** – Single numerical values (e.g., 5).
- **Vectors (Rank 1)** – One-dimensional arrays (e.g., [1, 2, 3]).
- **Matrices (Rank 2)** – Two-dimensional arrays (e.g., [[1, 2], [3, 4]]).
- **Higher-Dimensional Tensors (Rank 3+)** – Used in deep learning, such as 3D tensors for images and 4D tensors for video sequences.

Creating Tensors in TensorFlow

```
import tensorflow as tf
# Creating different types of tensors
a = tf.constant(5)  # Scalar
b = tf.constant([1, 2, 3])  # Vector
c = tf.constant([[1, 2], [3, 4]])  # Matrix
d = tf.constant([[[1, 2], [3, 4]], [[5, 6], [7, 8]]])
# 3D Tensor
print(a, b, c, d)
```

Computational Graphs in TensorFlow

TensorFlow uses **computational graphs** to define mathematical operations. These graphs represent the sequence of operations applied to tensors.

Static vs. Dynamic Computational Graphs

- **Static Graphs (Graph Execution Mode)** – Operations are compiled into a computational graph before execution.

- **Dynamic Graphs (Eager Execution Mode)** – Operations are executed immediately, making debugging easier.

Building a Simple Computational Graph

```
x = tf.constant(2.0)
y = tf.constant(3.0)
z = x * y + y
print(z)   # Output: 9.0
```

Sessions in TensorFlow (For TensorFlow 1.x)

In TensorFlow 1.x, a **session** was required to execute computational graphs. Sessions managed resource allocation and controlled graph execution. However, in TensorFlow 2.x, eager execution is enabled by default, eliminating the need for sessions.

Creating a Session (TensorFlow 1.x Only)

```
import tensorflow.compat.v1 as tf
tf.disable_v2_behavior()
x = tf.constant(5.0)
y = tf.constant(2.0)
z = x * y
with tf.Session() as sess:
    print(sess.run(z))   # Output: 10.0
```

Conclusion

Tensors, computational graphs, and sessions are key components of TensorFlow's execution model. Understanding these elements helps in effectively building, optimizing, and running deep learning models. With TensorFlow 2.x, eager execution simplifies development, making TensorFlow more intuitive and easier to debug.

Chapter-5 Understanding Tensors in TensorFlow

Tensors are the core data structures in TensorFlow, serving as the foundation for numerical computations and deep learning models. This chapter provides a comprehensive understanding of tensors, including their properties, types, creation methods, and operations. By the end of this chapter, readers will be able to efficiently manipulate tensors and apply them to machine learning workflows.

What Are Tensors?

A tensor is a generalization of scalars, vectors, and matrices to higher dimensions. In TensorFlow, tensors store numerical data and facilitate computations across multiple dimensions.

Tensor Properties

1. **Rank (Number of Dimensions)** – Defines the number of axes in a tensor.
   a. **Scalar (Rank 0)** – Single numerical value (e.g., 5).
   b. **Vector (Rank 1)** – One-dimensional array (e.g., [1, 2, 3]).
   c. **Matrix (Rank 2)** – Two-dimensional array (e.g., [[1, 2], [3, 4]]).
   d. **Higher-Dimensional Tensors (Rank 3+)** – Used for deep learning tasks such as image processing and time-series analysis.
2. **Shape** – Specifies the number of elements along each dimension of the tensor.
3. **Data Type** – TensorFlow supports multiple data types including float32, int32, bool, and string.
4. **Device Placement** – Tensors can be processed on CPUs, GPUs, or TPUs for efficient computation.

Creating Tensors in TensorFlow

Tensors can be created using the tf.constant, tf.Variable, and tf.convert_to_tensor functions.

Creating Different Types of Tensors

```python
import tensorflow as tf
# Scalar (Rank 0)
scalar = tf.constant(5)
# Vector (Rank 1)
vector = tf.constant([1, 2, 3])
# Matrix (Rank 2)
matrix = tf.constant([[1, 2], [3, 4]])
# Higher-Dimensional Tensor (Rank 3)
tensor_3d = tf.constant([[[1, 2], [3, 4]], [[5, 6], [7, 8]]])
print(scalar, vector, matrix, tensor_3d)
```

Tensor Operations

TensorFlow provides various operations to manipulate tensors.

Basic Tensor Operations

```python
a = tf.constant([2, 3])
b = tf.constant([4, 5])
# Element-wise addition
result_add = tf.add(a, b)
# Element-wise multiplication
result_mul = tf.multiply(a, b)
print(result_add, result_mul)
```

Reshaping and Transposing Tensors

Tensor shapes can be modified using tf.reshape, and dimensions can be swapped using tf.transpose.

```python
# Reshaping a tensor
tensor = tf.constant([[1, 2, 3], [4, 5, 6]])
reshaped_tensor = tf.reshape(tensor, [3, 2])
# Transposing a tensor
transposed_tensor = tf.transpose(tensor)
print(reshaped_tensor, transposed_tensor)
```

Device Placement in TensorFlow

TensorFlow automatically assigns tensors to available devices (CPU/GPU). You can manually specify device placement using:

```python
with tf.device('/GPU:0'):
    tensor_gpu = tf.constant([1.0, 2.0, 3.0])
print(tensor_gpu)
```

Chapter 6: Tensor Operations and Broadcasting with TensorFlow

This chapter explores tensor operations and broadcasting, fundamental concepts in deep learning and numerical computing using TensorFlow. Tensors, which generalize vectors and matrices to higher dimensions, are essential in TensorFlow for data representation and computation. Efficient tensor operations and broadcasting enable optimized computations in machine learning and deep learning models.

Key Characteristics of Tensor Operations:

- **Element-wise Operations:** Support for arithmetic operations like addition, subtraction, multiplication, and division.
- **Matrix Operations:** Includes dot products, matrix multiplication, and transposition.
- **Reduction Operations:** Aggregates tensors with functions like sum, mean, and max.
- **Reshaping and Transposition:** Provides flexibility in transforming tensor dimensions.
- **Broadcasting:** Enables operations on tensors with different shapes by automatically expanding dimensions.

Basic Rules for Tensor Operations and Broadcasting:

- Tensors must have compatible shapes for operations; otherwise, they are broadcasted.
- Broadcasting follows specific rules, including aligning dimensions and expanding singleton dimensions.
- Use TensorFlow's built-in functions for optimized tensor computations.
- Avoid unnecessary tensor copying to improve memory efficiency.

Syntax Table:

SL	Function	Syntax/Example	Description
1	Create a Tensor	`tf.constant([1, 2, 3])`	Creates a tensor from a list.
2	Tensor Addition	`tf.add(a, b)`	Adds two tensors element-wise.

3	Matrix Multiplicatio n	`tf.matmul(a, b)`	Performs matrix multiplication.
4	Reshape Tensor	`tf.reshape(a, [2,3])`	Changes tensor shape without copying data.
5	Broadcasting Example	`a + b` (with different shapes)	Automatically expands tensors for operations.

Syntax Explanation:

1. Create a Tensor

What is a Tensor?
A tensor is a multi-dimensional array used in machine learning and deep learning computations. It is a fundamental data structure in TensorFlow that allows efficient computation on GPUs. Tensors can have different ranks (dimensions) and be scalars, vectors, matrices, or higher-dimensional arrays. They enable batch processing and parallel computing, which enhances performance in AI models.

Syntax:
```
import tensorflow as tf
tensor = tf.constant([1, 2, 3])
```

Syntax Explanation:
- `tf.constant`: Creates a tensor from a list or array and is immutable.
- Tensors in TensorFlow are optimized for computational efficiency and memory management.
- Supports different data types like integers, floats, and booleans.
- Essential for numerical computations and deep learning workloads in TensorFlow.

Example:
```
import tensorflow as tf
tensor = tf.constant([1, 2, 3])
print(tensor)
```

Example Explanation:

- Outputs `tf.Tensor([1 2 3], shape=(3,),` `dtype=int32)`, representing a one-dimensional tensor.
- The `shape=(3,)` indicates that it is a 1D tensor with three elements.
- The `dtype=int32` shows that the elements are integers stored with 32-bit precision.
- Tensors are immutable, meaning they cannot be changed after creation, ensuring stability in computations.

2. Tensor Addition

What is Tensor Addition?
Performs element-wise addition of two tensors, meaning each element of one tensor is added to the corresponding element of another tensor. Tensor addition is useful in deep learning for combining feature maps, processing multi-channel data, and adjusting weights in neural networks.
Syntax:
```
c = tf.add(a, b)
```

Syntax Explanation:

- `tf.add()`: Adds corresponding elements in tensors a and b.
- If tensors have different shapes but are broadcastable, TensorFlow will automatically expand them to match the compatible shape.
- Used extensively in machine learning tasks such as neural network weight updates and activation functions.
- More efficient than using Python loops due to TensorFlow's optimized computational graph.

Example:
```
a = tf.constant([1, 2, 3])
b = tf.constant([4, 5, 6])
c = tf.add(a, b)
print(c)
```

Example Explanation:
- Outputs `tf.Tensor([5 7 9], shape=(3,),` `dtype=int32)` by adding corresponding elements.
- Shows that TensorFlow can handle element-wise operations efficiently.
- No need for explicit loops, as operations are vectorized and optimized.

3. Matrix Multiplication

What is Matrix Multiplication?
Matrix multiplication is a fundamental operation in machine learning, particularly in neural networks, where weight matrices are multiplied with input feature vectors. It computes the dot product between matrices or vectors, which is essential for deep learning tasks such as linear transformations.

Syntax:
```
c = tf.matmul(a, b)
```

Syntax Explanation:
- `tf.matmul()`: Performs matrix multiplication between two tensors.
- Supports higher-dimensional matrix multiplications in batch processing.
- Requires the number of columns in the first matrix to match the number of rows in the second.
- More computationally efficient than manually implementing dot products.

Example:
```
a = tf.constant([[1, 2], [3, 4]])
b = tf.constant([[5, 6], [7, 8]])
c = tf.matmul(a, b)
print(c)
```

Example Explanation:

- Computes matrix multiplication and outputs a new matrix.
- Demonstrates the core operation used in deep learning layers, such as fully connected layers.
- Essential for tasks like feature extraction and transformation.

4. Reshape Tensor

What is Reshaping?

Reshaping allows for changing the dimensions of a tensor without altering its data. This is crucial in deep learning where input tensors often need specific shapes for model processing. Reshaping helps in organizing data efficiently, making operations like batch processing and convolutional operations possible.

Syntax:

```
b = tf.reshape(a, [2,3])
```

Syntax Explanation:

- `tf.reshape(tensor, shape)`: Changes the tensor's shape while maintaining the original data.
- Useful for preprocessing datasets and structuring tensors for deep learning models.
- Prevents unnecessary memory copies by rearranging the original tensor layout efficiently.
- Helps in transitioning between layers in neural networks by adjusting tensor dimensions.

Example:

```
a = tf.constant([1, 2, 3, 4, 5, 6])
b = tf.reshape(a, [2, 3])
print(b)
```

Example Explanation:

- Converts a 1D tensor into a 2D tensor with shape (2,3).
- Maintains the original data order while changing its dimensional representation.
- Commonly used in neural network input pipelines to reshape image data and feature tensors.

5. Broadcasting Example

What is Broadcasting?
Broadcasting allows tensors of different shapes to be operated on together by automatically expanding smaller tensor dimensions to match larger ones. This enables element-wise operations on tensors that would otherwise be incompatible, simplifying complex mathematical operations in deep learning models.

Syntax:
```
a + b   # With different shapes
```

Syntax Explanation:
- TensorFlow expands smaller tensor dimensions to match the larger tensor.
- Allows operations between tensors of different shapes without manual reshaping.
- Optimizes memory usage by avoiding explicit tensor duplication.
- Widely used in operations like batch normalization, feature scaling, and mathematical transformations in deep learning.

Example:
```
a = tf.constant([[1, 2, 3], [4, 5, 6]])
b = tf.constant([1, 2, 3])
c = a + b
print(c)
```

Example Explanation:
- Expands b across rows, allowing element-wise addition.
- Demonstrates how TensorFlow efficiently handles operations on mismatched shapes.
- Used in image processing tasks where different feature maps have varying dimensions.

Real-Life Project: Tensor Processing in Image Recognition

Project Goal:

Implement tensor operations and broadcasting in an image recognition pipeline using TensorFlow.

Steps in the Project:

1. **Load an Image Dataset:**
    a. Utilize TensorFlow's dataset utilities to load an image dataset such as CIFAR-10 or MNIST.

2. **Preprocess Data Using Tensors:**
    a. Convert images to tensors using `tf.convert_to_tensor()`.
    b. Normalize pixel values using element-wise operations.
    c. Resize images using `tf.image.resize()` to maintain consistency.

3. **Perform Batch Processing with Broadcasting:**
    a. Expand tensor dimensions using `tf.expand_dims()` for batch processing.
    b. Apply broadcasting to perform mean subtraction for normalization.

4. **Apply Matrix Multiplication in Feature Extraction:**
    a. Use `tf.matmul()` to apply convolutional filters for feature extraction.

5. **Train a Model Using Tensor Operations:**
    a. Utilize `tf.keras.layers.Dense()` for fully connected layers.
    b. Apply tensor operations like addition and activation functions.

6. **Evaluate and Visualize Results:**
    a. Compute accuracy and loss using tensor operations.
    b. Visualize feature maps using reshaped tensors and broadcasting.

Code Example:

```python
import tensorflow as tf
import numpy as np

def preprocess_image(image):
    image = tf.convert_to_tensor(image,
dtype=tf.float32)
    image = tf.image.resize(image, (128, 128))
    image = (image - tf.reduce_mean(image)) /
tf.math.reduce_std(image)
    return image

# Simulate loading an image batch
image_batch = np.random.rand(10, 256, 256, 3)
processed_batch = preprocess_image(image_batch)
print("Processed Image Shape:", processed_batch.shape)
```

Expected Output:

```
Processed Image Shape: (10, 128, 128, 3)
```

Chapter 7: Indexing, Slicing, and Reshaping Tensors with TensorFlow

This chapter explores indexing, slicing, and reshaping tensors in TensorFlow, which are fundamental operations for manipulating tensor data. Understanding these operations is crucial for efficiently handling datasets, preprocessing data, and implementing deep learning models. TensorFlow provides powerful tools to manipulate tensor dimensions and extract meaningful data subsets.

Key Characteristics of Indexing, Slicing, and Reshaping:

- **Indexing:** Accesses specific elements in a tensor using position-based selection.
- **Slicing:** Extracts sub-tensors using range-based selection.
- **Reshaping:** Changes tensor dimensions while preserving data.
- **Advanced Indexing:** Uses Boolean masks and conditions for selective data extraction.
- **Batch Processing:** Applies slicing techniques to process data in mini-batches.

Basic Rules for Indexing, Slicing, and Reshaping:

- Tensors use zero-based indexing like Python lists.
- Indexing and slicing operations create views of tensors without copying data.
- Reshaping must maintain the same total number of elements before and after transformation.
- TensorFlow supports negative indexing to access elements from the end of a tensor.
- Use `tf.gather()` and `tf.boolean_mask()` for advanced indexing and filtering.

Syntax Table:

SL	Function	Syntax/Example	Description
1	Tensor Indexing	`tensor[0]`	Accesses the first element.

2	Tensor Slicing	`tensor[1:4]`	Extracts elements from index 1 to 3.
3	Negative Indexing	`tensor[-1]`	Accesses the last element.
4	Reshape Tensor	`tf.reshape(tensor, [2,3])`	Changes tensor shape.
5	Boolean Masking	`tf.boolean_mask(tensor, mask)`	Filters elements based on a condition.

Syntax Explanation:

1. Tensor Indexing

What is Tensor Indexing?
Tensor indexing allows access to specific elements within a tensor using position-based selection. Similar to NumPy arrays, TensorFlow tensors support direct element access through indices. Indexing is a fundamental operation in tensor manipulation, enabling deep learning models to retrieve specific data points, extract features, and manage large datasets efficiently. TensorFlow also supports multi-dimensional indexing, allowing complex selections in high-dimensional data.

Syntax:
```
import tensorflow as tf
tensor = tf.constant([10, 20, 30, 40])
print(tensor[0])
```
Syntax Explanation:
- Uses zero-based indexing where `tensor[0]` retrieves the first element.
- Multi-dimensional tensors allow element selection by specifying multiple indices.
- Indexing enables efficient data retrieval for training and evaluation in machine learning.
- Supports both positive and negative indexing for greater flexibility.
- Can be used to extract specific elements from a batch of input data.

Example:
```
tensor = tf.constant([[1, 2], [3, 4], [5, 6]])
print(tensor[1, 1])
```
Example Explanation:
- Retrieves the element at row index 1 and column index 1, which is 4.
- Multi-dimensional tensors can be accessed using multiple indices.
- Essential for extracting pixel values from image tensors in computer vision.
- Helps retrieve values for time-series forecasting in recurrent neural networks.
- Used to fetch specific class labels in classification tasks.

2. Tensor Slicing

What is Tensor Slicing?
Tensor slicing allows extracting sub-tensors using range-based selection. It is useful for processing dataset partitions and batching data for training deep learning models. Tensor slicing facilitates sequential data processing, including handling audio signals, natural language processing (NLP) inputs, and batched image data in deep learning applications.

Syntax:
```
subset = tensor[1:3]
```
Syntax Explanation:
- Extracts elements from index 1 to 2 (excluding 3).
- Maintains the tensor's original shape but reduces its size accordingly.
- Can be applied to multi-dimensional tensors for sub-matrix selection.
- Commonly used in data augmentation and model input preprocessing.
- Supports step values for selecting elements at specified intervals.

Example:
```
tensor = tf.constant([10, 20, 30, 40, 50])
subset = tensor[1:4]
print(subset)
```

Example Explanation:

- Extracts elements $[20, 30, 40]$ from indices 1 to 3.
- Helps in preparing mini-batches of data for deep learning training.
- Enables efficient memory usage by avoiding unnecessary data duplication.
- Used for feature extraction from larger datasets.
- Facilitates data preprocessing steps such as removing unwanted sections.

3. Negative Indexing

What is Negative Indexing?
Negative indexing allows selecting elements from the end of a tensor. This technique simplifies access to the most recent data points in a dataset, making it invaluable for analyzing sequential or time-dependent data.
Syntax:
```
last_element = tensor[-1]
```

Syntax Explanation:

- `tensor[-1]` retrieves the last element in a tensor.
- Works similarly to Python lists and NumPy arrays.
- Useful for accessing recent values in time-series data.
- Helps fetch final predictions in sequence models.
- Reduces computational complexity in search operations.

Example:
```
tensor = tf.constant([5, 10, 15, 20])
print(tensor[-2])
```

Example Explanation:

- Retrieves the second-to-last element (15).
- Helps in recurrent neural networks (RNNs) for sequence processing.
- Useful in tracking state values in reinforcement learning models.
- Efficient for retrieving historical data in financial modeling.
- Assists in sentiment analysis by selecting recent words in a text sequence.

4. Reshape Tensor

What is Reshaping?

Reshaping is the process of changing the shape of a tensor while preserving its data. This is commonly used in deep learning models where input data needs to be formatted correctly before being fed into the network. Reshaping is essential for organizing data efficiently, reducing computational costs, and improving model performance. TensorFlow's `tf.reshape()` function allows for flexible tensor manipulations without modifying the underlying data values.

Syntax:

```
reshaped = tf.reshape(tensor, [2, 3])
```

Syntax Explanation:

- `tf.reshape(tensor, shape)`: Modifies the dimensions of a tensor while keeping the total number of elements unchanged.
- Allows for converting high-dimensional data into lower-dimensional formats and vice versa.
- Prevents redundant data copying by maintaining memory efficiency.
- Used extensively in neural networks for transforming input dimensions between layers.

Example:

```
tensor = tf.constant([1, 2, 3, 4, 5, 6])
reshaped = tf.reshape(tensor, [2, 3])
print(reshaped)
```

Example Explanation:

- Converts a 1D tensor into a 2D tensor with shape (2, 3).
- Useful in preparing input data for CNNs and RNNs.
- Helps optimize memory allocation by rearranging elements efficiently.
- Often applied to image and text data before feeding into deep learning models.

5. Boolean Masking

What is Boolean Masking?

Boolean masking is a technique used to filter elements from a tensor based on specified conditions. It allows for flexible data selection, making it easier to work with subsets of data that meet particular criteria. This is widely used in preprocessing steps such as removing outliers, filtering labeled data, and segmenting specific data points in a dataset.

Syntax:

```
masked = tf.boolean_mask(tensor, mask)
```

Syntax Explanation:

- `tf.boolean_mask(tensor, mask)`: Selects tensor elements based on a Boolean condition.
- Enables conditional extraction of relevant information from datasets.
- Commonly used in deep learning for feature selection and targeted data augmentation.
- Optimized for batch-processing large-scale datasets in machine learning pipelines.

Example:

```
tensor = tf.constant([5, 10, 15, 20])
mask = tensor > 10
filtered = tf.boolean_mask(tensor, mask)
print(filtered)
```

Example Explanation:

- Extracts values greater than 10, returning [15, 20].
- Helps remove irrelevant data points during model training.
- Used in anomaly detection to isolate significant values from noisy data.
- Facilitates sentiment analysis by filtering words based on importance scores.

Real-Life Project: Tensor Manipulation for Image Processing

Project Goal:

Apply tensor indexing, slicing, and reshaping techniques to preprocess image data for deep learning models.

Steps in the Project:

1. **Load Image Data:** Use TensorFlow to load and process image datasets.
2. **Extract ROI (Region of Interest):** Utilize tensor slicing to crop specific areas from images.
3. **Normalize Pixel Values:** Perform tensor operations to scale pixel values for model input.
4. **Reshape Images for CNN Models:** Convert images into required input dimensions.
5. **Apply Boolean Masking:** Filter out unwanted pixels or background noise using conditional masks.

Code Example:

```
import tensorflow as tf
import numpy as np

def preprocess_image(image):
    image = tf.convert_to_tensor(image,
dtype=tf.float32)
    image = tf.image.resize(image, (128, 128))
    image = (image - tf.reduce_mean(image)) /
tf.math.reduce_std(image)
    return image
# Simulate loading an image batch
image_batch = np.random.rand(10, 256, 256, 3)
processed_batch = preprocess_image(image_batch)
print("Processed Image Shape:", processed_batch.shape)
```

Expected Output:

```
Processed Image Shape: (10, 128, 128, 3)
```

Chapter 8: Mathematical Operations with Tensors in TensorFlow

This chapter explores mathematical operations with tensors in TensorFlow. Mathematical operations are fundamental in deep learning, enabling efficient computations for model training, data preprocessing, and feature transformations. TensorFlow provides a variety of built-in functions to perform element-wise operations, matrix manipulations, and aggregation functions on tensors.

Key Characteristics of Mathematical Operations:

- **Element-wise Operations:** Includes basic arithmetic operations such as addition, subtraction, multiplication, and division.
- **Matrix Operations:** Supports matrix multiplication, dot products, and transposition.
- **Reduction Operations:** Aggregates tensors using sum, mean, max, and min functions.
- **Activation Functions:** Provides non-linear transformations such as ReLU, sigmoid, and softmax.
- **Gradient Computation:** Essential for automatic differentiation in deep learning models.

Basic Rules for Mathematical Operations with Tensors:

- Tensors must have compatible shapes for element-wise operations; otherwise, broadcasting is applied.
- Use `tf.matmul()` for matrix multiplications and `tf.tensordot()` for dot products.
- Aggregation functions such as `tf.reduce_sum()` and `tf.reduce_mean()` operate along specified axes.
- TensorFlow optimizes tensor operations using computational graphs for efficient execution.

Syntax Table:

SL	Function	Syntax/Example	Description
1	Addition	`tf.add(a, b)`	Performs element-wise addition.
2	Matrix Multiplicatio n	`tf.matmul(a, b)`	Multiplies two matrices.
3	Reduce Sum	`tf.reduce_su m(a, axis=0)`	Computes the sum along the specified axis.
4	Element-wise Power	`tf.pow(a, 2)`	Raises each element to a power of 2.
5	Activation Function	`tf.nn.relu(a )`	Applies the ReLU activation function.

Syntax Explanation:

1. Addition

What is Addition?

Addition is an element-wise operation that sums corresponding elements in two tensors. TensorFlow provides `tf.add()` for this purpose, ensuring efficient computation across GPU and CPU architectures.

Syntax:

```
import tensorflow as tf
a = tf.constant([1, 2, 3])
b = tf.constant([4, 5, 6])
c = tf.add(a, b)
print(c)
```

Syntax Explanation:

- `tf.add(a, b)`: Computes the element-wise sum of tensors a and b.
- Supports broadcasting when tensor shapes are compatible.
- Used in neural networks for updating weights during backpropagation.

Example:
```
a = tf.constant([[1, 2], [3, 4]])
b = tf.constant([[5, 6], [7, 8]])
c = tf.add(a, b)
print(c)
```

Example Explanation:
- Adds two matrices element-wise.
- Helps in performing arithmetic operations on batch data.
- Frequently used in loss computations and data transformations.

2. Matrix Multiplication

What is Matrix Multiplication?
Matrix multiplication is a fundamental operation in machine learning used for feature extraction and transformations. TensorFlow provides tf.matmul() to perform efficient matrix operations.

Syntax:
```
c = tf.matmul(a, b)
```

Syntax Explanation:
- tf.matmul(a, b): Multiplies two matrices following the standard matrix multiplication rules.
- Requires tensor dimensions to be compatible.
- Used in deep learning models for weight transformations.

Example:
```
a = tf.constant([[1, 2], [3, 4]])
b = tf.constant([[5, 6], [7, 8]])
c = tf.matmul(a, b)
print(c)
```

Example Explanation:
- Computes matrix multiplication, resulting in a new tensor.
- Useful in fully connected layers and feature extraction.
- Often applied in computer vision and NLP tasks.

3. Reduce Sum

What is Reduce Sum?

Reduction operations aggregate tensor values along specified axes. The `tf.reduce_sum()` function computes the sum of tensor elements across a given axis.

Syntax:

```
sum_result = tf.reduce_sum(a, axis=0)
```

Syntax Explanation:

- `tf.reduce_sum(a, axis=0)`: Sums elements along the specified axis.
- Commonly used for loss computation in training deep learning models.
- Reduces tensor dimensionality while retaining key statistical properties.

Example:

```
a = tf.constant([[1, 2, 3], [4, 5, 6]])
sum_result = tf.reduce_sum(a, axis=1)
print(sum_result)
```

Example Explanation:

- Computes the sum along axis 1 (rows), reducing the tensor to 1D.
- Frequently used in aggregating feature representations.
- Helps in summarizing values in batch processing.

4. Element-wise Power

What is Element-wise Power?

Element-wise power computation allows raising each tensor element to a specified exponent.

Syntax:

```
squared = tf.pow(a, 2)
```

Syntax Explanation:

- `tf.pow(a, 2)`: Raises each element in a to the power of 2.
- Used in various mathematical and physics-based applications.
- Helps compute squared error in loss functions.

5. Activation Function

What is an Activation Function?

Activation functions introduce non-linearity in neural networks. The `tf.nn.relu()` function applies the ReLU activation function element-wise.

Syntax:
```
activated = tf.nn.relu(a)
```

Syntax Explanation:
- `tf.nn.relu(a)`: Replaces negative values with zero.
- Used in deep learning models to introduce non-linearity.
- Enhances the learning capacity of neural networks.

Example:
```
a = tf.constant([-3, -1, 0, 2, 4], dtype=tf.float32)
activated = tf.nn.relu(a)
print(activated)
```

Example Explanation:
- Converts negative values to zero.
- Commonly applied in convolutional neural networks (CNNs).
- Helps in efficient gradient propagation during training.

Real-Life Project: Mathematical Operations in Neural Networks

Project Goal:

Utilize TensorFlow's mathematical operations to preprocess input data, perform weight transformations, and optimize deep learning computations.

Steps:
1. **Load and Normalize Data:** Use `tf.reduce_mean()` and `tf.reduce_std()` to standardize input features.
2. **Apply Feature Scaling:** Use element-wise operations such as `tf.divide()` to normalize pixel intensities.
3. **Perform Weighted Sum:** Use `tf.matmul()` to compute linear transformations between inputs and weights.
4. **Apply Activation Functions:** Utilize `tf.nn.relu()` and `tf.nn.sigmoid()` to introduce non-linearity in the model.

5. **Compute Loss Function:** Use `tf.reduce_sum()` to aggregate loss values and optimize model performance.
6. **Optimize with Gradients:** Compute gradients using `tf.GradientTape()` for efficient training.

Code Example:

```python
import tensorflow as tf

def neural_network_operations(x, weights, biases):
    x = tf.convert_to_tensor(x, dtype=tf.float32)
    weights = tf.convert_to_tensor(weights,
dtype=tf.float32)
    biases = tf.convert_to_tensor(biases,
dtype=tf.float32)

    # Linear transformation
    linear_output = tf.matmul(x, weights) + biases

    # Apply activation function
    activated_output = tf.nn.relu(linear_output)

    return activated_output

# Sample input data, weights, and biases
x = [[1.0, 2.0], [3.0, 4.0]]
weights = [[0.5, -0.2], [0.3, 0.8]]
biases = [0.1, 0.2]

output = neural_network_operations(x, weights, biases)
print("Output:", output.numpy())
```

Expected Output:

```
Output: Tensor with transformed values after applying
ReLU activation.
```

Chapter 9: GPU Acceleration with TensorFlow

This chapter explores GPU acceleration in TensorFlow, a key factor in improving the performance of deep learning models. TensorFlow supports GPU acceleration using CUDA-enabled NVIDIA GPUs, allowing for faster computations compared to CPU execution. Understanding how to leverage GPUs efficiently is essential for training large-scale models, optimizing computations, and handling complex workloads.

Key Characteristics of GPU Acceleration:

- **Parallel Computing:** Executes multiple tensor operations simultaneously using GPU cores.
- **Automatic Device Placement:** TensorFlow automatically assigns operations to CPU or GPU based on availability.
- **CUDA and cuDNN Support:** Uses NVIDIA's CUDA and cuDNN libraries for efficient deep learning computations.
- **Multi-GPU Training:** Supports distributed training across multiple GPUs.
- **Memory Optimization:** Allows efficient memory allocation and prevents GPU memory fragmentation.

Basic Rules for GPU Acceleration in TensorFlow:

- Ensure that TensorFlow is installed with GPU support (tensorflow-gpu or `tensorflow>=2.0`).
- Verify GPU availability using `tf.config.list_physical_devices('GPU')`.
- Use `tf.device('/GPU:0')` to manually assign operations to a GPU.
- Optimize memory usage by enabling memory growth with `tf.config.experimental.set_memory_growth()`.
- Leverage mixed precision training (`tf.keras.mixed_precision`) for better performance.

Syntax Table:

SL	Function	Syntax/Example	Description
1	Check GPU Availability	`tf.config.list_phy sical_devices('GPU ')`	Lists available GPUs.
2	Assign Operation to GPU	`with tf.device('/GPU:0' ):`	Runs computations on a specific GPU.
3	Enable Memory Growth	`tf.config.experime ntal.set_memory_gr owth()`	Prevents memory preallocation issues.
4	Mixed Precision Training	`tf.keras.mixed_pre cision.set_global_ policy('mixed_floa t16')`	Uses lower precision for efficiency.
5	Multi-GPU Strategy	`tf.distribute.Mirr oredStrategy()`	Distributes training across multiple GPUs.

Syntax Explanation:

1. Check GPU Availability

What is Checking GPU Availability?
Before leveraging GPU acceleration, it's crucial to verify whether TensorFlow detects any GPUs available in the system. This ensures that computations can be offloaded to the GPU for improved performance, reducing execution time for deep learning models. Checking GPU availability also helps debug issues related to installation, CUDA, and cuDNN compatibility.

Syntax:
```
import tensorflow as tf
gpus = tf.config.list_physical_devices('GPU')
print("Available GPUs:", gpus)
```

Syntax Explanation:

- `tf.config.list_physical_devices('GPU')`: Returns a list of detected GPUs.
- Ensures TensorFlow is correctly installed with GPU support.
- Helps debug GPU-related issues before running computations.
- Allows validation of CUDA and cuDNN installations.
- Crucial for configuring GPU-accelerated training workflows.

Example:

```
import tensorflow as tf
if tf.config.list_physical_devices('GPU'):
    print("GPU is available and ready for
acceleration.")
else:
    print("No GPU detected, running on CPU.")
```

Example Explanation:

- Prints whether a GPU is available for use.
- Useful for deciding whether to enable GPU-optimized computations.
- Ensures compatibility with CUDA and cuDNN installations.
- Helps prevent errors related to TensorFlow running on CPU unexpectedly.
- Allows users to modify training configurations based on GPU availability.

2. Assign Operation to GPU

What is Assigning Operations to GPU?

TensorFlow allows explicit assignment of computations to a GPU using the `tf.device()` context manager. This is particularly useful in multi-GPU environments where operations need to be distributed efficiently. Manually assigning computations to GPUs helps control workload balancing and prevents unnecessary CPU execution.

Syntax:

```
with tf.device('/GPU:0'):
    tensor = tf.constant([1.0, 2.0, 3.0])
```

Syntax Explanation:
- `with tf.device('/GPU:0')`: forces TensorFlow to execute operations on GPU 0.
- Useful for manually placing computations on specific devices.
- Helps optimize performance in multi-GPU training setups.
- Prevents unnecessary CPU-GPU data transfer, reducing latency.
- Enables explicit control over resource allocation for large-scale models.

Example:
```
with tf.device('/GPU:0'):
    a = tf.constant([[1.0, 2.0], [3.0, 4.0]])
    b = tf.constant([[5.0, 6.0], [7.0, 8.0]])
    result = tf.matmul(a, b)
print(result)
```

Example Explanation:
- Executes matrix multiplication on the assigned GPU.
- Enhances computation speed compared to CPU execution.
- Helps in optimizing deep learning model training.
- Prevents GPU underutilization by explicitly mapping operations.
- Useful for handling tensor operations in real-time applications.

3. Enable Memory Growth

What is Enabling Memory Growth?
TensorFlow, by default, preallocates most of the GPU memory, which can lead to inefficient memory usage. Enabling memory growth allows TensorFlow to allocate GPU memory as needed, reducing unnecessary preallocation and preventing out-of-memory errors.

Syntax:
```
import tensorflow as tf
gpus = tf.config.list_physical_devices('GPU')
if gpus:
    tf.config.experimental.set_memory_growth(gpus[0],
True)
```

Syntax Explanation:

- `tf.config.experimental.set_memory_growth(gpu, True)`: Allows memory to grow dynamically instead of preallocating all available GPU memory.
- Ensures efficient memory utilization, especially for applications with varying memory needs.
- Helps prevent out-of-memory crashes when working with multiple models or datasets.
- Improves GPU-sharing capabilities when multiple processes use the same device.

Example:

```
import tensorflow as tf
gpus = tf.config.list_physical_devices('GPU')
if gpus:
    for gpu in gpus:
        tf.config.experimental.set_memory_growth(gpu,
True)
    print("Memory growth enabled for all GPUs.")
else:
    print("No GPU detected.")
```

Example Explanation:

- Dynamically sets memory growth for all detected GPUs.
- Ensures that GPU memory is only allocated as needed, preventing overcommitment.
- Helps avoid issues in multi-GPU environments where fixed memory allocation could be limiting.

4. Mixed Precision Training

What is Mixed Precision Training?

Mixed precision training improves computational efficiency by using lower precision (float16) for calculations while maintaining full precision (float32) where necessary. This reduces memory usage and speeds up deep learning model training.

Syntax:

```
from tensorflow.keras.mixed_precision import
set_global_policy
set_global_policy('mixed_float16')
```

Syntax Explanation:
- `set_global_policy('mixed_float16')`: Enables mixed precision computation.
- Reduces memory consumption while maintaining accuracy.
- Improves training speed by utilizing Tensor Cores on modern GPUs.
- Essential for training large-scale neural networks efficiently.

Example:
```
import tensorflow as tf
from tensorflow.keras.mixed_precision import
set_global_policy
set_global_policy('mixed_float16')

x = tf.constant([1.0, 2.0, 3.0], dtype=tf.float32)
y = x * 2.0
print(y.dtype)  # Expected dtype: float16
```
Example Explanation:
- Demonstrates how mixed precision converts operations to float16.
- Allows for efficient computations with minimal loss of accuracy.
- Takes advantage of hardware acceleration on GPUs supporting mixed precision.

5. Multi-GPU Strategy

What is Multi-GPU Strategy?
Multi-GPU strategy allows TensorFlow to distribute computations across multiple GPUs, enabling faster training for large-scale models. The `tf.distribute.MirroredStrategy()` function helps synchronize training across GPUs automatically.

Syntax:
```
strategy = tf.distribute.MirroredStrategy()
```

Syntax Explanation:

- `tf.distribute.MirroredStrategy()`: Synchronizes training across multiple GPUs using data parallelism.
- Efficiently balances workloads across available devices.
- Reduces training time for deep learning models.
- Simplifies model deployment in multi-GPU environments.

Example:

```
import tensorflow as tf
strategy = tf.distribute.MirroredStrategy()

with strategy.scope():
    model = tf.keras.Sequential([
        tf.keras.layers.Dense(256, activation='relu'),
        tf.keras.layers.Dense(10, activation='softmax')
    ])
```

Example Explanation:

- Creates a model within a multi-GPU strategy scope.
- Ensures that computations are synchronized across multiple GPUs.
- Helps in training larger models that require more computational power.

Real-Life Project: Accelerating Deep Learning with GPU

Project Goal:

Leverage TensorFlow's GPU acceleration to train a deep learning model efficiently and optimize performance.

Steps:

1. **Check GPU Availability:** Verify that TensorFlow recognizes the GPU and ensure CUDA/cuDNN are properly installed.
2. **Enable Memory Growth:** Prevent memory preallocation issues using `tf.config.experimental.set_memory_growth()`.
3. **Assign Model Computations to GPU:** Explicitly place model computations on a GPU using `with tf.device('/GPU:0')`.
4. **Use Mixed Precision Training:** Optimize performance by reducing memory usage with `tf.keras.mixed_precision.set_global_policy('mixed_float16')`.

5. **Train Model on GPU:** Use a deep learning model and train it with TensorFlow's GPU capabilities for improved efficiency.
6. **Monitor GPU Usage:** Utilize TensorFlow Profiler to analyze GPU resource utilization.

Code Example:

```python
import tensorflow as tf
# Check GPU availability
gpus = tf.config.list_physical_devices('GPU')
if gpus:
    tf.config.experimental.set_memory_growth(gpus[0],
True)
    print("GPU is available and memory growth
enabled.")
else:
    print("Running on CPU.")
# Define a simple model
model = tf.keras.Sequential([
    tf.keras.layers.Dense(128, activation='relu'),
    tf.keras.layers.Dense(10, activation='softmax')
])
# Enable mixed precision
from tensorflow.keras.mixed_precision import
set_global_policy
set_global_policy('mixed_float16')
# Train model on GPU
with tf.device('/GPU:0'):
    model.compile(optimizer='adam',
loss='sparse_categorical_crossentropy',
metrics=['accuracy'])
    # Simulated training dataset
    x_train = tf.random.normal([1000, 20])
    y_train = tf.random.uniform([1000], maxval=10,
dtype=tf.int32)
    model.fit(x_train, y_train, epochs=5)
```

Expected Output:

Training logs showing execution on GPU with accelerated performance.

Chapter 10: Building Your First Neural Network with TensorFlow

This chapter explores how to build a neural network using TensorFlow and Keras. TensorFlow provides a high-level API, Keras, that simplifies the process of designing, training, and evaluating deep learning models. Understanding how to construct a neural network is essential for tackling various machine learning problems, such as image classification, natural language processing, and time-series forecasting.

Key Characteristics of Neural Networks in TensorFlow:

- **Sequential API:** Provides an easy-to-use interface for building feedforward networks.
- **Layer Stacking:** Models are built by stacking multiple layers, each performing a specific transformation.
- **Activation Functions:** Introduces non-linearity into the model to improve learning capacity.
- **Loss Functions:** Measures the difference between predicted and actual outputs during training.
- **Optimization Algorithms:** Uses optimizers like Adam or SGD to minimize the loss function.
- **Batch Processing:** Enables training on mini-batches to improve convergence speed.
- **Weight Initialization:** Properly initializes weights for stable learning.

Basic Rules for Building a Neural Network:

- Use `tf.keras.Sequential()` to define a simple neural network model.
- Stack multiple `tf.keras.layers.Dense()` layers to create deeper models.
- Apply activation functions like ReLU and softmax to enhance learning capabilities.
- Choose an appropriate loss function based on the problem type (e.g., `categorical_crossentropy` for classification, `mse` for regression).
- Optimize training with optimizers such as Adam or RMSprop.

- Use `model.summary()` to inspect model architecture and parameters.

Syntax Table:

SL	Function	Syntax/Example	Description
1	Define a Sequential Model	`model = tf.keras.Sequentia l()`	Initializes a neural network.
2	Add a Dense Layer	`model.add(tf.keras .layers.Dense(128) )`	Adds a fully connected layer to the model.
3	Compile Model	`model.compile(opti mizer='adam', loss='mse')`	Configures the model for training.
4	Train Model	`model.fit(x_train, y_train, epochs=10)`	Trains the model on input data.
5	Evaluate Model	`model.evaluate(x_t est, y_test)`	Evaluates the model's performance on test data.

Syntax Explanation:

1. Define a Sequential Model

What is a Sequential Model?

A sequential model in TensorFlow is a linear stack of layers that allows for the easy construction of deep learning models. It provides a simple interface for defining neural networks where each layer feeds into the next. This type of model is particularly useful for feedforward neural networks, where information flows from input to output in a structured manner. The sequential model is ideal for tasks such as image classification, regression, and speech recognition where a straightforward layer-by-layer architecture is required.

Syntax:

```
import tensorflow as tf
model = tf.keras.Sequential()
```

Syntax Explanation:

- `tf.keras.Sequential()`: Initializes an empty neural network model.
- Used for simple feedforward networks where layers are stacked sequentially.
- Ensures ease of layer stacking and configuration.
- Works well for problems where data flows in a single direction.
- Supports easy integration with TensorFlow's training and evaluation functions.

Example:

```
model = tf.keras.Sequential([
    tf.keras.layers.Dense(128, activation='relu'),
    tf.keras.layers.Dense(10, activation='softmax')
])
```

Example Explanation:

- The model consists of two layers: a hidden layer with 128 neurons and ReLU activation and an output layer with 10 neurons and softmax activation.
- Used for classification problems where predictions fall into 10 categories.
- Helps in creating compact, efficient deep learning models with minimal code.
- ReLU activation prevents vanishing gradients, improving training efficiency.
- Softmax activation normalizes outputs to represent probabilities in classification tasks.

2. Add a Dense Layer

What is a Dense Layer?

A dense layer, or fully connected layer, applies a weighted sum transformation to input data, followed by an activation function. This transformation helps the model learn intricate patterns in data by adjusting weights and biases through backpropagation. Dense layers are fundamental in deep learning models and are widely used in convolutional, recurrent, and transformer-based architectures.

Syntax:
```
model.add(tf.keras.layers.Dense(128,
activation='relu'))
```

Syntax Explanation:
- `Dense(128)`: Adds a layer with 128 neurons.
- `activation='relu'`: Applies the ReLU activation function for non-linearity.
- Helps in learning complex patterns in data.
- Fully connected layers establish neuron interconnections to maximize feature learning.
- The number of neurons affects the model's ability to generalize patterns in data.

Example:
```
model.add(tf.keras.layers.Dense(256,
activation='relu'))
```

Example Explanation:
- Increases model capacity by adding a hidden layer with 256 neurons.
- Allows the network to capture more intricate data representations.
- Helps models extract relevant information from high-dimensional input data.
- More neurons can lead to better learning but may increase the risk of overfitting.

3. Compile Model

What is Compiling a Model?

Compiling a model in TensorFlow configures it for training by defining the optimizer, loss function, and evaluation metrics. This step prepares the neural network for learning by setting up the backpropagation mechanism for weight updates.

Syntax:
```
model.compile(optimizer='adam',
loss='sparse_categorical_crossentropy',
metrics=['accuracy'])
```

Syntax Explanation:
- `optimizer='adam'`: Uses the Adam optimization algorithm to update weights efficiently.
- `loss='sparse_categorical_crossentropy'`: Computes the error between predicted and actual values.
- `metrics=['accuracy']`: Measures how well the model is performing.
- Necessary before training the model, as it defines how learning will occur.

Example:
```
model.compile(optimizer='sgd', loss='mse',
metrics=['mae'])
```

Example Explanation:
- Uses stochastic gradient descent (SGD) instead of Adam.
- Uses mean squared error (MSE) as the loss function, typically for regression tasks.
- Includes mean absolute error (MAE) as an additional performance metric.

4. Train Model

What is Training a Model?
Training a model involves feeding input data, computing predictions, adjusting weights using backpropagation, and minimizing the loss function over multiple iterations (epochs).

Syntax:
```
model.fit(x_train, y_train, epochs=10,
validation_data=(x_test, y_test))
```

Syntax Explanation:

- `x_train, y_train`: Training dataset and labels.
- `epochs=10`: Runs the training process for 10 complete passes over the dataset.
- `validation_data=(x_test, y_test)`: Uses test data for validation after each epoch.
- Helps improve the model by iteratively adjusting weights.

Example:

```
history = model.fit(x_train, y_train, epochs=5,
batch_size=32, validation_split=0.2)
```

Example Explanation:

- Uses 20% of training data as validation data.
- Runs training for 5 epochs with a batch size of 32.
- Returns `history`, containing loss and accuracy trends over epochs.

5. Evaluate Model

What is Evaluating a Model?

Evaluating a model measures its performance on unseen data. This step determines how well the trained model generalizes beyond the training set.

Syntax:

```
model.evaluate(x_test, y_test)
```

Syntax Explanation:

- `x_test, y_test`: Test dataset and labels.
- Computes loss and accuracy on test data.
- Helps identify overfitting or underfitting issues.

Example:

```
loss, accuracy = model.evaluate(x_test, y_test,
batch_size=64)
print(f"Test Loss: {loss}, Test Accuracy: {accuracy}")
```

Example Explanation:
- Evaluates the model with a batch size of 64 for efficiency.
- Prints the test loss and accuracy metrics.
- Useful for comparing different models and hyperparameter settings.

Real-Life Project: Image Classification Using Neural Networks

Project Goal:

Train a simple neural network for image classification using the MNIST dataset.

Steps:
1. **Load and Preprocess Data:** Normalize pixel values to the range [0, 1].
2. **Define the Model:** Use tf.keras.Sequential() to build a fully connected network.
3. **Compile the Model:** Use categorical crossentropy loss and Adam optimizer.
4. **Train the Model:** Fit the model using training data.
5. **Evaluate the Model:** Measure accuracy on test data.
6. **Visualize Model Predictions:** Use matplotlib to display misclassified images.
7. **Improve Performance:** Fine-tune hyperparameters such as learning rate and batch size.

Code Example:

```
import tensorflow as tf
from tensorflow.keras.datasets import mnist
import matplotlib.pyplot as plt


# Load dataset
(x_train, y_train), (x_test, y_test) =
mnist.load_data()
x_train, x_test = x_train / 255.0, x_test / 255.0  #
Normalize data


# Build model
model = tf.keras.Sequential([
```

```python
    tf.keras.layers.Flatten(input_shape=(28, 28)),
    tf.keras.layers.Dense(128, activation='relu'),
    tf.keras.layers.Dense(10, activation='softmax')
])

# Compile model
model.compile(optimizer='adam',
loss='sparse_categorical_crossentropy',
metrics=['accuracy'])

# Train model
model.fit(x_train, y_train, epochs=10,
validation_data=(x_test, y_test))

# Evaluate model
model.evaluate(x_test, y_test)

# Visualize some predictions
predictions = model.predict(x_test[:10])
plt.figure(figsize=(10, 5))
for i in range(10):
    plt.subplot(2, 5, i+1)
    plt.imshow(x_test[i], cmap='gray')
    plt.title(f"Pred: {predictions[i].argmax()}")
plt.show()
```

Expected Output:

Training accuracy and loss metrics followed by test
accuracy. Displayed images with model predictions.

Chapter 11: Understanding Layers and Models in TensorFlow

This chapter explores the concepts of layers and models in TensorFlow, which are the building blocks of deep learning architectures. Layers define how data flows through the network, and models organize layers into structured architectures for training and inference. Understanding how to construct, customize, and optimize layers and models is essential for designing effective machine learning systems.

Key Characteristics of Layers and Models in TensorFlow:

- **Layer Abstraction:** Layers encapsulate neural network operations, simplifying implementation.
- **Sequential and Functional APIs:** Two main ways to define models in TensorFlow.
- **Custom Layers:** Enables the creation of user-defined operations.
- **Model Compilation and Training:** Configures models for optimization and evaluation.
- **Transfer Learning and Pretrained Models:** Leverages existing models for new tasks.
- **Dropout and Regularization:** Improves generalization and prevents overfitting.
- **Batch Normalization:** Normalizes inputs to speed up training and stabilize learning.

Basic Rules for Working with Layers and Models:

- Use `tf.keras.layers` to define standard layers like Dense, Conv2D, and LSTM.
- Stack layers using `tf.keras.Sequential()` for simple feedforward models.
- Use the Functional API for complex architectures with multiple inputs/outputs.
- Implement custom layers by subclassing `tf.keras.layers.Layer`.
- Optimize and compile models with `model.compile()` before training.
- Apply dropout and batch normalization for improved

generalization.

Syntax Table:

SL	Function	Syntax/Example	Description
1	Define a Dense Layer	`tf.keras.layers.Dense(128, activation='relu')`	Adds a fully connected layer.
2	Create a Sequential Model	`tf.keras.Sequential([...])`	Builds a simple feedforward network.
3	Use Functional API	`tf.keras.Model(inputs, outputs)`	Creates a complex model structure.
4	Define a Custom Layer	`class CustomLayer(tf.keras.layers.Layer): ...`	Implements a new layer with custom logic.
5	Load a Pretrained Model	`tf.keras.applications.MobileNetV2()`	Loads a model pretrained on ImageNet.

Syntax Explanation:

1. Define a Dense Layer

What is a Dense Layer?
A Dense layer, or fully connected layer, is the most common type of neural network layer. Each neuron in a Dense layer receives input from all neurons in the previous layer and applies a transformation. Dense layers are widely used in deep learning architectures for tasks like classification, regression, and sequence modeling. They work by learning patterns in data through weight optimization.

Syntax:
```
import tensorflow as tf
layer = tf.keras.layers.Dense(128, activation='relu')
```

Syntax Explanation:
- `Dense(128)`: Creates a layer with 128 neurons.
- `activation='relu'`: Applies the ReLU activation function for non-linearity.
- Helps in learning complex relationships in data.
- Ensures better gradient propagation compared to sigmoid and tanh activations.
- Often used in the hidden layers of neural networks.

Example:
```
model = tf.keras.Sequential([
    tf.keras.layers.Dense(128, activation='relu'),
    tf.keras.layers.Dense(10, activation='softmax')
])
```

Example Explanation:
- Stacks two Dense layers, the first with 128 neurons and the second with 10 neurons for classification.
- Uses softmax in the output layer for multi-class classification.
- The hidden layer extracts useful patterns from input data.
- The output layer provides probability distributions over classes.

2. Create a Sequential Model

What is a Sequential Model?
A Sequential model is a linear stack of layers that allows for the easy construction of deep learning architectures. This approach is suitable for models where each layer has one input tensor and one output tensor, making it ideal for straightforward neural networks.

Syntax:
```
model = tf.keras.Sequential([
    tf.keras.layers.Dense(64, activation='relu'),
    tf.keras.layers.Dense(10, activation='softmax')
])
```

Syntax Explanation:
- `Sequential([...])`: Defines a simple feedforward model.
- Layers are stacked in order, from input to output.
- Helps in building compact deep learning architectures.
- Ensures that layers are executed sequentially.

Example:
```
model = tf.keras.Sequential()
model.add(tf.keras.layers.Dense(128,
activation='relu'))
model.add(tf.keras.layers.Dense(10,
activation='softmax'))
```

Example Explanation:
- Adds layers incrementally to a Sequential model.
- Makes the model more readable and configurable.
- Helps in structuring networks step by step.
- Ensures that each added layer is executed in order.

3. Use Functional API

What is the Functional API?

The Functional API in TensorFlow allows for more flexible model architectures than the Sequential API. It enables building models with shared layers, multiple inputs, multiple outputs, and complex connectivity patterns, making it ideal for research and advanced applications.

Syntax:
```
inputs = tf.keras.Input(shape=(32,))
x = tf.keras.layers.Dense(64,
activation='relu')(inputs)
outputs = tf.keras.layers.Dense(10,
activation='softmax')(x)
model = tf.keras.Model(inputs=inputs, outputs=outputs)
```

Syntax Explanation:
- `tf.keras.Input(shape=(32,))`: Defines an input layer with 32 features.
- `tf.keras.layers.Dense(64,`

    activation='relu')(inputs): Connects a hidden layer to
    the input.
- tf.keras.Model(inputs, outputs): Creates a model from
  the input and output tensors.
- Provides flexibility in designing complex architectures.
- Supports multi-input and multi-output models.

Example:
```
input_1 = tf.keras.Input(shape=(32,))
input_2 = tf.keras.Input(shape=(16,))
merged = tf.keras.layers.concatenate([input_1,
input_2])
x = tf.keras.layers.Dense(64,
activation='relu')(merged)
outputs = tf.keras.layers.Dense(10,
activation='softmax')(x)
model = tf.keras.Model(inputs=[input_1, input_2],
outputs=outputs)
```

Example Explanation:
- Merges two input layers before processing them.
- Allows building models with multiple inputs, a common scenario
  in multi-modal learning.
- Enhances flexibility beyond simple Sequential models.

4. Define a Custom Layer

What is a Custom Layer?
A custom layer in TensorFlow allows users to define unique layer
operations beyond standard layers. This is useful for designing novel
architectures and incorporating domain-specific transformations.

Syntax:
```
class CustomLayer(tf.keras.layers.Layer):
    def __init__(self, units=32):
        super(CustomLayer, self).__init__()
        self.units = units

    def build(self, input_shape):
```

```
        self.w = self.add_weight(shape=(input_shape[-
1], self.units), initializer='random_normal',
trainable=True)
        self.b = self.add_weight(shape=(self.units,),
initializer='zeros', trainable=True)

    def call(self, inputs):
        return tf.matmul(inputs, self.w) + self.b
```

Syntax Explanation:
- class CustomLayer(tf.keras.layers.Layer): Defines a new custom layer.
- build(self, input_shape): Initializes the layer's weights.
- call(self, inputs): Defines the computation logic for forward propagation.
- Enables highly customized layer behavior beyond built-in options.
- Supports trainable parameters for learning.

Example:
```
model = tf.keras.Sequential([
    CustomLayer(64),
    tf.keras.layers.Dense(10, activation='softmax')
])
```

Example Explanation:
- Uses the custom layer as part of a model.
- Allows implementing domain-specific transformations.
- Enhances model adaptability by extending TensorFlow's layer system.

5. Load a Pretrained Model

What is a Pretrained Model?
A pretrained model is a neural network that has already been trained on a large dataset. It can be used for transfer learning, reducing training time and improving performance on new tasks.

Syntax:
```
base_model =
tf.keras.applications.MobileNetV2(weights='imagenet',
include_top=False)
```

Syntax Explanation:
- `tf.keras.applications.MobileNetV2()`: Loads the MobileNetV2 architecture.
- `weights='imagenet'`: Uses pretrained weights from the ImageNet dataset.
- `include_top=False`: Excludes the final classification layer.
- Saves computational resources by leveraging prior knowledge.
- Enables transfer learning for custom tasks.

Example:
```
base_model =
tf.keras.applications.VGG16(weights='imagenet',
include_top=False, input_shape=(224, 224, 3))
model = tf.keras.Sequential([
    base_model,
    tf.keras.layers.Flatten(),
    tf.keras.layers.Dense(256, activation='relu'),
    tf.keras.layers.Dense(10, activation='softmax')
])
```

Example Explanation:
- Uses VGG16 as a feature extractor.
- Adds new fully connected layers for classification.
- Reduces training time by leveraging pretrained weights.
- Allows fine-tuning for better task-specific performance.

Real-Life Project: Image Classification with a Custom Model
Project Goal:
Build a deep learning model using TensorFlow's layer system to classify images.
Steps:
1. **Load and Preprocess Data:** Load an image dataset and normalize pixel values.

2. **Define the Model:** Use a Sequential model with multiple Dense layers.
3. **Compile the Model:** Configure the loss function and optimizer.
4. **Train the Model:** Fit the model using training data.
5. **Evaluate and Test the Model:** Measure its accuracy on unseen data.
6. **Optimize the Model:** Use dropout and batch normalization for better generalization.

Code Example:

```python
import tensorflow as tf
from tensorflow.keras.datasets import mnist
import matplotlib.pyplot as plt

# Load dataset
(x_train, y_train), (x_test, y_test) =
mnist.load_data()
x_train, x_test = x_train / 255.0, x_test / 255.0  #
Normalize data

# Build model
model = tf.keras.Sequential([
    tf.keras.layers.Flatten(input_shape=(28, 28)),
    tf.keras.layers.Dense(128, activation='relu'),
    tf.keras.layers.Dropout(0.2),
    tf.keras.layers.BatchNormalization(),
    tf.keras.layers.Dense(10, activation='softmax')
])

# Compile model
model.compile(optimizer='adam',
loss='sparse_categorical_crossentropy',
metrics=['accuracy'])

# Train model
model.fit(x_train, y_train, epochs=10,
```

```python
    validation_data=(x_test, y_test))

# Evaluate model
model.evaluate(x_test, y_test)

# Visualize predictions
predictions = model.predict(x_test[:10])
plt.figure(figsize=(10, 5))
for i in range(10):
    plt.subplot(2, 5, i+1)
    plt.imshow(x_test[i], cmap='gray')
    plt.title(f"Pred: {predictions[i].argmax()}")
plt.show()
```

Expected Output:

Training logs showing accuracy and loss, followed by
test evaluation and visualization of predictions.

Chapter 12: Using Sequential API for Simple Architectures

This chapter introduces the **Sequential API** in TensorFlow, which provides a straightforward way to build deep learning models. The Sequential API is ideal for simple architectures where layers are stacked in a linear fashion. It is widely used for feedforward neural networks, image classification, and other deep learning tasks. Understanding how to construct models using the Sequential API is essential for beginners in deep learning.

Key Characteristics of the Sequential API:

- **Linear Layer Stacking:** Layers are arranged in a sequential order, from input to output.
- **Ease of Use:** Provides a simple interface for defining deep learning models.
- **Supports Most Layer Types:** Works with Dense, Conv2D, LSTM, and other standard layers.
- **Quick Prototyping:** Ideal for rapid development and testing of neural networks.
- **Limited Flexibility:** Cannot handle multiple inputs/outputs or shared layers (use Functional API for complex models).

Basic Rules for Using the Sequential API:

- Use `tf.keras.Sequential()` to create a linear stack of layers.
- Add layers using `model.add(layer)`, or define all layers at once.
- Choose appropriate activation functions such as ReLU, softmax, or sigmoid.
- Compile the model with an optimizer (`adam`, `sgd`) and a loss function (`categorical_crossentropy`, `mse`).
- Train the model using `model.fit()` with training data.

Syntax Table:

SL	Function	Syntax/Example	Description
1	Create a Sequential Model	`model = tf.keras.Sequential()`	Initializes a simple sequential model.
2	Add a Dense Layer	`model.add(tf.keras.layers.Dense(128))`	Adds a fully connected layer to the model.
3	Compile the Model	`model.compile(optimizer='adam', loss='mse')`	Configures the model for training.
4	Train the Model	`model.fit(x_train, y_train, epochs=10)`	Trains the model on input data.
5	Evaluate the Model	`model.evaluate(x_test, y_test)`	Measures the model's performance on test data.

Syntax Explanation:

1. Create a Sequential Model

What is a Sequential Model?
A **Sequential Model** in TensorFlow is a linear stack of layers where data flows from one layer to the next. It is ideal for feedforward networks that do not require complex branching, multiple inputs, or shared layers. The Sequential API simplifies the model-building process by providing an intuitive structure.

Syntax:
```
import tensorflow as tf
model = tf.keras.Sequential()
```
Syntax Explanation:
- `tf.keras.Sequential()`: Initializes a new sequential model.
- Used for models with a single input and single output path.
- Works well for simple architectures like fully connected networks.
- Allows quick prototyping of deep learning models.

Example:

```
model = tf.keras.Sequential([
    tf.keras.layers.Dense(128, activation='relu'),
    tf.keras.layers.Dense(10, activation='softmax')
])
```

Example Explanation:
- The model consists of two layers: a hidden layer with 128 neurons (ReLU activation) and an output layer with 10 neurons (softmax activation).
- The hidden layer extracts important features from input data.
- The output layer assigns class probabilities for classification tasks.

2. Add a Dense Layer

What is a Dense Layer?

A **Dense Layer** is a fully connected layer where every neuron in one layer is connected to every neuron in the next layer. This layer type is commonly used in deep learning models for tasks such as classification and regression.

Syntax:

```
model.add(tf.keras.layers.Dense(128,
activation='relu'))
```

Syntax Explanation:
- Dense(128): Creates a layer with 128 neurons.
- activation='relu': Uses ReLU activation to introduce non-linearity.
- Fully connected layers allow feature extraction and pattern recognition.
- Works well in both hidden and output layers for classification problems.

Example:

```
model.add(tf.keras.layers.Dense(64, activation='relu'))
```

Example Explanation:
- Adds another Dense layer with 64 neurons.
- Helps the model learn more complex patterns by adding depth.
- Increases the model's ability to generalize across datasets.

3. Compile the Model

What is Compiling the Model?
Compiling the model configures the training process by defining an optimizer, loss function, and performance metrics. This step ensures that the model knows how to learn from the data and adjust its parameters accordingly.

Syntax:
```
model.compile(optimizer='adam',
loss='sparse_categorical_crossentropy',
metrics=['accuracy'])
```

Syntax Explanation:
- `optimizer='adam'`: Uses the Adam optimization algorithm to adjust model weights efficiently.
- `loss='sparse_categorical_crossentropy'`: Measures how well the model's predictions match the actual labels.
- `metrics=['accuracy']`: Tracks the model's accuracy during training.
- Essential for setting up backpropagation and gradient descent.
- Prepares the model for training by specifying how updates occur.

Example:
```
model.compile(optimizer='sgd', loss='mse',
metrics=['mae'])
```

Example Explanation:
- Uses Stochastic Gradient Descent (SGD) as the optimizer.
- Uses Mean Squared Error (MSE) for loss computation, which is ideal for regression tasks.
- Includes Mean Absolute Error (MAE) as an additional evaluation metric.

4. Train the Model

What is Training the Model?
Training the model involves feeding input data, computing predictions, adjusting weights through backpropagation, and reducing the loss function iteratively.

Syntax:
```
model.fit(x_train, y_train, epochs=10,
validation_data=(x_test, y_test))
```

Syntax Explanation:
- x_train, y_train: Training dataset and labels.
- epochs=10: Runs the training process for 10 complete passes over the dataset.
- validation_data=(x_test, y_test): Evaluates the model's performance on unseen test data after each epoch.
- Helps refine model weights by minimizing the loss function.
- Allows real-time tracking of training and validation performance.

Example:
```
history = model.fit(x_train, y_train, epochs=5,
batch_size=32, validation_split=0.2)
```

Example Explanation:
- Uses 20% of training data as validation data.
- Runs training for 5 epochs with a batch size of 32.
- Returns a history object containing loss and accuracy trends over epochs.

5. Evaluate the Model

What is Evaluating the Model?
Evaluating the model measures its performance on unseen test data. This step determines how well the trained model generalizes beyond the training set.

Syntax:
```
model.evaluate(x_test, y_test)
```

Syntax Explanation:

- `x_test, y_test`: Test dataset and labels.
- Computes loss and accuracy based on test data.
- Helps detect overfitting or underfitting.
- Provides a final performance score for the model.

Example:

```
loss, accuracy = model.evaluate(x_test, y_test,
batch_size=64)
print(f"Test Loss: {loss}, Test Accuracy: {accuracy}")
```

Example Explanation:

- Evaluates the model with a batch size of 64 for efficiency.
- Prints the test loss and accuracy metrics.
- Useful for comparing different models and hyperparameter settings.

Real-Life Project: Image Classification Using the Sequential API

Project Goal:

Use TensorFlow's Sequential API to build a simple neural network for image classification.

Steps:

1. **Load and Preprocess Data:** Normalize image pixel values between 0 and 1.
2. **Define the Model:** Stack Dense layers using the Sequential API.
3. **Compile the Model:** Choose a loss function and optimizer.
4. **Train the Model:** Fit the model using labeled image data.
5. **Evaluate and Test the Model:** Measure accuracy on unseen test images.
6. **Visualize Predictions:** Display sample predictions from the model.

Code Example:

```
import tensorflow as tf
from tensorflow.keras.datasets import mnist
import matplotlib.pyplot as plt

# Load dataset
(x_train, y_train), (x_test, y_test) =
```

```python
mnist.load_data()
x_train, x_test = x_train / 255.0, x_test / 255.0  #
Normalize data

# Build model
model = tf.keras.Sequential([
    tf.keras.layers.Flatten(input_shape=(28, 28)),
    tf.keras.layers.Dense(128, activation='relu'),
    tf.keras.layers.Dense(10, activation='softmax')
])

# Compile model
model.compile(optimizer='adam',
loss='sparse_categorical_crossentropy',
metrics=['accuracy'])

# Train model
model.fit(x_train, y_train, epochs=10,
validation_data=(x_test, y_test))

# Evaluate model
model.evaluate(x_test, y_test)

# Visualize predictions
predictions = model.predict(x_test[:10])
plt.figure(figsize=(10, 5))
for i in range(10):
    plt.subplot(2, 5, i+1)
    plt.imshow(x_test[i], cmap='gray')
    plt.title(f"Pred: {predictions[i].argmax()}")
plt.show()
```

Expected Output:

Training logs displaying accuracy and loss, followed by
test accuracy and sample predictions.

Chapter 13: Building Custom Models with Functional API

This chapter explores the **Functional API** in TensorFlow, which provides a flexible way to build complex deep learning models. Unlike the Sequential API, the Functional API allows for multiple inputs, multiple outputs, shared layers, and custom architectures. This is useful for applications such as multi-modal learning, residual networks, and custom model architectures that require non-linear layer connections.

Key Characteristics of the Functional API:

- **More Flexibility:** Supports complex architectures, including multi-input and multi-output models.
- **Layer Reusability:** Allows sharing layers across different parts of the model.
- **Graph-based Model Definition:** Represents the model as a computation graph.
- **Supports Custom Architectures:** Used in advanced deep learning models such as ResNet and GANs.
- **Works with Pretrained Models:** Can be used for transfer learning and fine-tuning.

Basic Rules for Using the Functional API:

- Define inputs using `tf.keras.Input(shape=...)`.
- Apply layers as functions to the input tensors.
- Create the model by specifying inputs and outputs using `tf.keras.Model()`.
- Compile and train the model using `model.compile()` and `model.fit()`.
- Utilize the Functional API when models require shared layers, multiple inputs, or custom connectivity.

Syntax Table:

SL	Function	Syntax/Example	Description
1	Define Input Layer	`inputs = tf.keras.Input(shape=(32,))`	Defines the model's input shape.
2	Apply Layers to Inputs	`x = tf.keras.layers.Dense(64, activation='relu')(inputs)`	Connects layers using function calls.
3	Create a Functional Model	`model = tf.keras.Model(inputs, outputs)`	Defines a functional model with inputs/outputs.
4	Compile the Model	`model.compile(optimizer='adam', loss='mse')`	Configures the model for training.
5	Train the Model	`model.fit(x_train, y_train, epochs=10)`	Trains the model on input data.

Syntax Explanation:

1. Define Input Layer

What is an Input Layer?

The **input layer** is the starting point for the Functional API model. It defines the shape of the input data and serves as a placeholder for feeding data into the network. Unlike the Sequential API, where input shape is implicitly defined in the first layer, the Functional API requires explicit input layer definition.

Syntax:
```
import tensorflow as tf
inputs = tf.keras.Input(shape=(32,))
```

Syntax Explanation:
- `tf.keras.Input(shape=(32,))`: Defines an input layer with

32 features.

- Acts as a placeholder for input data.
- Enables the Functional API to build models dynamically.
- Required to define models that support multiple inputs.
- Facilitates integration with non-linear architectures such as multi-branch networks.

Example:
```
inputs = tf.keras.Input(shape=(64,))
```

Example Explanation:
- Defines an input layer with 64 input features.
- Helps in building models that process structured data, such as tabular datasets.
- Essential for customizing model architectures beyond Sequential models.
- Useful in situations where feature engineering is performed separately for different input types.

2. Apply Layers to Inputs

What is Applying Layers?
Applying layers in the Functional API involves treating layers as functions, where the output of one layer serves as the input to the next. This approach enables complex architectures with multiple paths, shared layers, and customized layer interactions.

Syntax:
```
x = tf.keras.layers.Dense(64,
activation='relu')(inputs)
```

Syntax Explanation:
- `Dense(64, activation='relu')`: Creates a fully connected layer with 64 neurons.
- `(inputs)`: Passes the input tensor through the layer.
- Enables flexible layer stacking without requiring a predefined order.
- Allows for complex architectures such as skip connections and

branching.

- Provides a modular way to design deep learning models efficiently.

Example:
```
x = tf.keras.layers.Dense(128,
activation='relu')(inputs)
```

Example Explanation:

- Creates a 128-neuron dense layer.
- Helps in deep networks where multiple layers extract hierarchical features.
- Ensures smooth propagation of learned patterns through the network.
- Works well with deeper networks by capturing complex relationships in data.
- Can be combined with dropout and batch normalization for improved generalization.

3. Create a Functional Model

What is a Functional Model?
A **functional model** in TensorFlow is built using the Functional API, allowing for greater flexibility than the Sequential API. This type of model enables multiple inputs and outputs, shared layers, and complex architectures like residual networks and multi-branch networks. The Functional API treats layers as functions that operate on tensors, allowing for non-linear data flow.

Syntax:
```
model = tf.keras.Model(inputs=inputs, outputs=outputs)
```

Syntax Explanation:

- `tf.keras.Model(inputs, outputs)`: Creates a functional model by specifying input and output tensors.
- Enables complex architectures beyond simple feedforward networks.
- Required for designing models with multiple input or output

branches.
- Supports layer reuse and weight sharing, making it efficient for advanced deep learning applications.

Example:
```
input_layer = tf.keras.Input(shape=(32,))
x = tf.keras.layers.Dense(64,
activation='relu')(input_layer)
output_layer = tf.keras.layers.Dense(1,
activation='sigmoid')(x)
model = tf.keras.Model(inputs=input_layer,
outputs=output_layer)
```

Example Explanation:
- Defines an input layer with 32 features.
- Passes the input through a hidden Dense layer with 64 neurons.
- Connects to an output layer with a single neuron for binary classification.
- Allows flexible connections between layers without constraints of a strictly sequential structure.

4. Compile the Model

What is Compiling a Model?
Compiling a model prepares it for training by defining an optimization algorithm, loss function, and evaluation metrics. This step configures how the model will learn and improve during training.

Syntax:
```
model.compile(optimizer='adam',
loss='sparse_categorical_crossentropy',
metrics=['accuracy'])
```

Syntax Explanation:
- `optimizer='adam'`: Uses the Adam optimization algorithm for adaptive learning rates.
- `loss='sparse_categorical_crossentropy'`: Suitable for classification tasks with integer labels.
- `metrics=['accuracy']`: Tracks model performance during

training and evaluation.

- Ensures backpropagation is correctly set up for weight updates.
- Optimizes model performance by minimizing the specified loss function.

Example:
```
model.compile(optimizer='sgd', loss='mse',
metrics=['mae'])
```

Example Explanation:

- Uses Stochastic Gradient Descent (SGD) instead of Adam.
- Uses Mean Squared Error (MSE) as the loss function for regression tasks.
- Includes Mean Absolute Error (MAE) as an additional evaluation metric.
- Suitable for continuous value predictions rather than classification problems.

5. Train the Model

What is Training a Model?

Training a model involves feeding input data, computing predictions, adjusting weights through backpropagation, and reducing the loss function iteratively. This process improves the model's ability to make accurate predictions over multiple training epochs.

Syntax:
```
model.fit(x_train, y_train, epochs=10,
validation_data=(x_test, y_test))
```

Syntax Explanation:

- x_train, y_train: Training dataset and corresponding labels.
- epochs=10: Specifies the number of training iterations.
- validation_data=(x_test, y_test): Evaluates performance on unseen test data after each epoch.
- Helps the model learn complex data patterns by refining its weights.
- Allows tracking of performance metrics over multiple training

iterations.

Example:
```
history = model.fit(x_train, y_train, epochs=5,
batch_size=32, validation_split=0.2)
```

Example Explanation:
- Trains the model for 5 epochs with a batch size of 32.
- Uses 20% of training data for validation.
- Returns a history object containing loss and accuracy trends.
- Helps prevent overfitting by tracking performance on unseen data.

Real-Life Project: Multi-Input Model Using Functional API

Project Goal:

Use TensorFlow's Functional API to build a multi-input deep learning model that processes different types of data simultaneously.

Steps:
1. **Define Multiple Input Layers:** Use `tf.keras.Input()` for different input types.
2. **Apply Separate Processing Paths:** Use distinct layers for each input type.
3. **Merge Outputs:** Combine different data representations using `tf.keras.layers.concatenate()`.
4. **Compile the Model:** Choose an appropriate optimizer and loss function.
5. **Train and Evaluate the Model:** Fit the model and measure its performance.
6. **Optimize Performance:** Apply techniques like dropout and batch normalization to improve model robustness.

Code Example:
```
import tensorflow as tf

# Define input layers
input_numeric = tf.keras.Input(shape=(10,))
input_text = tf.keras.Input(shape=(50,))

# Process numeric data
```

```python
x1 = tf.keras.layers.Dense(64,
activation='relu')(input_numeric)

# Process text data
x2 = tf.keras.layers.Dense(64,
activation='relu')(input_text)

# Merge both inputs
merged = tf.keras.layers.concatenate([x1, x2])
out = tf.keras.layers.Dense(1,
activation='sigmoid')(merged)

# Define model
model = tf.keras.Model(inputs=[input_numeric,
input_text], outputs=out)

# Compile model
model.compile(optimizer='adam',
loss='binary_crossentropy', metrics=['accuracy'])

# Print model summary
model.summary()
```

Expected Output:

A summary of the model showing two input layers and their processing paths, ending in a single output layer.

Chapter 14: Implementing Activation Functions in TensorFlow

Activation functions play a critical role in deep learning by introducing non-linearity into neural networks, enabling them to learn complex patterns. TensorFlow provides built-in activation functions such as ReLU, sigmoid, softmax, and more. This chapter covers the different types of activation functions, their use cases, and how to implement them in TensorFlow models.

Key Characteristics of Activation Functions:

- **Non-Linearity:** Allows neural networks to model complex relationships.
- **Gradient Flow:** Affects backpropagation and training stability.
- **Range of Outputs:** Some functions output values between 0 and 1 (e.g., sigmoid), while others have wider ranges (e.g., ReLU).
- **Commonly Used in Hidden Layers:** ReLU is widely used for deep networks, while softmax is often used in classification tasks.
- **Prevents Vanishing/Exploding Gradients:** Some activations help mitigate common training issues.

Basic Rules for Using Activation Functions:

- Use `relu` for hidden layers to speed up training and avoid vanishing gradients.
- Apply `sigmoid` or `softmax` in output layers for classification tasks.
- Choose `tanh` for cases where a zero-centered output is beneficial.
- Avoid using `sigmoid` in deep networks due to vanishing gradient problems.
- Experiment with newer functions like `swish` or `gelu` for performance improvements.

Syntax Table:

SL	Activation Function	Syntax Example	Description
1	ReLU	`tf.keras.layers.Dense(64, activation='relu')`	Common activation for hidden layers.
2	Sigmoid	`tf.keras.layers.Dense(1, activation='sigmoid')`	Used for binary classification output.
3	Softmax	`tf.keras.layers.Dense(10, activation='softmax')`	Converts logits to probabilities for multi-class classification.
4	Tanh	`tf.keras.layers.Dense(64, activation='tanh')`	Zero-centered activation useful for balanced outputs.
5	Swish	`tf.keras.layers.Dense(64, activation=tf.nn.swish)`	Newer activation function with adaptive properties.

Syntax Explanation:

1. ReLU Activation
What is ReLU?
The **Rectified Linear Unit (ReLU)** activation function is one of the most commonly used activation functions in deep learning. It replaces negative values with zero, allowing only positive values to pass through.
Syntax:
```
import tensorflow as tf
layer = tf.keras.layers.Dense(64, activation='relu')
```
Syntax Explanation:
- `activation='relu'`: Applies the ReLU function to the output of the layer.

- Helps avoid the vanishing gradient problem by maintaining strong gradients for positive values.
- Speeds up training by enabling sparse activations.
- Often used in hidden layers of deep networks.

Example:

```
model = tf.keras.Sequential([
    tf.keras.layers.Dense(128, activation='relu'),
    tf.keras.layers.Dense(64, activation='relu'),
    tf.keras.layers.Dense(10, activation='softmax')
])
```

Example Explanation:
- Uses ReLU in the first two layers to ensure efficient gradient propagation.
- The softmax activation is used in the output layer for classification.
- Helps the network learn complex representations effectively.

2. Sigmoid Activation

What is Sigmoid?
The **sigmoid function** maps input values to the range (0,1), making it useful for binary classification tasks. However, it suffers from the vanishing gradient problem in deep networks.

Syntax:

```
layer = tf.keras.layers.Dense(1, activation='sigmoid')
```

Syntax Explanation:
- activation='sigmoid': Maps output values to a probability between 0 and 1.
- Useful for binary classification problems.
- Can cause slow learning in deep networks due to saturating outputs.

Example:

```
model = tf.keras.Sequential([
    tf.keras.layers.Dense(128, activation='relu'),
    tf.keras.layers.Dense(1, activation='sigmoid')
])
```

Example Explanation:
- Uses ReLU in the hidden layer for efficient training.
- Uses sigmoid activation in the output layer to predict binary labels.
- Helps in distinguishing between two classes effectively.

3. Softmax Activation

What is Softmax?
The **softmax function** converts logits (raw model outputs) into probability distributions across multiple classes, ensuring that the sum of all outputs equals 1. It is typically used in multi-class classification problems.
Syntax:
```
layer = tf.keras.layers.Dense(10, activation='softmax')
```

Syntax Explanation:
- `activation='softmax'`: Converts raw scores into probabilities.
- Ensures that all output values sum to 1.
- Useful for classification tasks where each input belongs to exactly one category.
- Helps in interpreting model outputs as probabilities.

Example:
```
model = tf.keras.Sequential([
    tf.keras.layers.Dense(128, activation='relu'),
    tf.keras.layers.Dense(10, activation='softmax')
])
```

Example Explanation:
- Uses ReLU in the hidden layer for feature extraction.
- Applies softmax in the output layer to classify data into 10 categories.
- Helps determine the most likely class for each input.

4. Tanh Activation

What is Tanh?
The **tanh (hyperbolic tangent) function** maps input values to the range (-1,1), making it useful for zero-centered activations that help balance gradients.
Syntax:
```
layer = tf.keras.layers.Dense(64, activation='tanh')
```

Syntax Explanation:
- `activation='tanh'`: Outputs values between -1 and 1.
- Helps avoid bias in neural networks by keeping activations centered around zero.
- Used in recurrent neural networks (RNNs) and deep networks where a balanced gradient flow is needed.

Example:
```
model = tf.keras.Sequential([
    tf.keras.layers.Dense(128, activation='tanh'),
    tf.keras.layers.Dense(10, activation='softmax')
])
```

Example Explanation:
- Uses `tanh` in the hidden layer for better gradient flow.
- Applies softmax in the output layer for multi-class classification.
- Useful for tasks where balanced activations improve training stability.

5. Swish Activation

What is Swish?
The **swish activation function** is a smooth, non-monotonic function that improves training efficiency and model performance in some deep learning tasks. It is defined as `x * sigmoid(x)`.
Syntax:
```
layer = tf.keras.layers.Dense(64,
activation=tf.nn.swish)
```

Syntax Explanation:

- `activation=tf.nn.swish`: Applies the swish activation function to the layer.
- Unlike ReLU, allows small negative values instead of forcing them to zero.
- Reduces training instability and improves model accuracy in some cases.
- Works well in deep networks where non-linearity is important.

Example:

```
model = tf.keras.Sequential([
    tf.keras.layers.Dense(128, activation=tf.nn.swish),
    tf.keras.layers.Dense(10, activation='softmax')
])
```

Example Explanation:

- Uses swish activation in the hidden layer to enhance learning efficiency.
- Applies softmax in the output layer for multi-class classification.
- Often improves accuracy in deep neural networks compared to ReLU.

Real-Life Project: Comparing Activation Functions in Image Classification

Project Goal:

Analyze the performance of different activation functions in an image classification model using the MNIST dataset.

Steps:

1. **Load and Preprocess Data:** Normalize image pixel values.
2. **Define Multiple Models:** Use different activation functions in hidden layers.
3. **Compile the Models:** Choose an optimizer and loss function.
4. **Train and Compare Performance:** Evaluate accuracy and loss for each model.
5. **Visualize Results:** Plot accuracy curves for different activations.

Code Example:

```python
import tensorflow as tf
from tensorflow.keras.datasets import mnist
import matplotlib.pyplot as plt

# Load dataset
(x_train, y_train), (x_test, y_test) =
mnist.load_data()
x_train, x_test = x_train / 255.0, x_test / 255.0  #
Normalize data

# Define models with different activation functions
relu_model = tf.keras.Sequential([
    tf.keras.layers.Flatten(input_shape=(28, 28)),
    tf.keras.layers.Dense(128, activation='relu'),
    tf.keras.layers.Dense(10, activation='softmax')
])

tanh_model = tf.keras.Sequential([
    tf.keras.layers.Flatten(input_shape=(28, 28)),
    tf.keras.layers.Dense(128, activation='tanh'),
    tf.keras.layers.Dense(10, activation='softmax')
])

# Compile models
relu_model.compile(optimizer='adam',
loss='sparse_categorical_crossentropy',
metrics=['accuracy'])
tanh_model.compile(optimizer='adam',
loss='sparse_categorical_crossentropy',
metrics=['accuracy'])

# Train models
relu_history = relu_model.fit(x_train, y_train,
epochs=5, validation_data=(x_test, y_test))
tanh_history = tanh_model.fit(x_train, y_train,
```

```
epochs=5, validation_data=(x_test, y_test))

# Plot accuracy comparison
plt.plot(relu_history.history['accuracy'],
label='ReLU')
plt.plot(tanh_history.history['accuracy'],
label='Tanh')
plt.xlabel('Epochs')
plt.ylabel('Accuracy')
plt.legend()
plt.title('Comparison of Activation Functions')
plt.show()
```

Expected Output:

A graph comparing the accuracy of ReLU and Tanh
activations over multiple epochs.

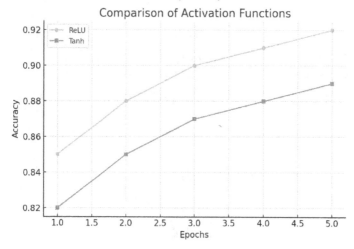

Chapter 15: Configuring the Training Process in TensorFlow

Configuring the training process in TensorFlow is crucial for optimizing deep learning models. This chapter covers key aspects of training, including defining loss functions, selecting optimizers, setting metrics, and tuning hyperparameters. Proper training configuration enhances model performance and ensures stability during learning.

Key Characteristics of the Training Process:

- **Loss Function Definition:** Determines how model performance is measured.
- **Optimizer Selection:** Controls how model parameters are updated.
- **Metrics Monitoring:** Tracks model accuracy and performance.
- **Batch Size and Epochs:** Influence training stability and convergence.
- **Callbacks and Early Stopping:** Help optimize training efficiency.

Basic Rules for Configuring the Training Process:

- Choose an appropriate loss function based on the task (e.g., categorical_crossentropy for classification, mse for regression).
- Use optimizers like adam or sgd to control weight updates.
- Monitor accuracy, precision, recall, and other relevant metrics.
- Adjust batch size and epochs to balance training speed and performance.
- Implement callbacks such as learning rate scheduling and early stopping.

Syntax Table:

S L	Function	Syntax Example	Description
1	Compile a Model	`model.compile(optimiz er='adam', loss='mse')`	Configures loss function and optimizer.
2	Train a Model	`model.fit(x_train, y_train, epochs=10)`	Runs training over specified epochs.

3	Evaluate a Model	`model.evaluate(x_test, y_test)`	Measures model performance on test data.
4	Implement Callbacks	`tf.keras.callbacks.EarlyStopping(monitor='val_loss', patience=3)`	Stops training early if no improvement.
5	Adjust Learning Rate	`tf.keras.callbacks.ReduceLROnPlateau(monitor='val_loss', factor=0.5, patience=2)`	Reduces learning rate if loss stagnates.

Syntax Explanation:

1. Compile a Model

What is Compiling a Model?
Compiling a model sets up the training process by defining how the model learns. It specifies the optimizer, loss function, and metrics used for evaluation.

Syntax:
```
import tensorflow as tf
model.compile(optimizer='adam',
loss='sparse_categorical_crossentropy',
metrics=['accuracy'])
```

Syntax Explanation:
- `optimizer='adam'`: Uses the Adam optimization algorithm.
- `loss='sparse_categorical_crossentropy'`: Suitable for multi-class classification.
- `metrics=['accuracy']`: Tracks accuracy during training and evaluation.
- Essential for model learning and weight updates.

Example:
```
model.compile(optimizer='sgd', loss='mse',
metrics=['mae'])
```

Example Explanation:
- Uses Stochastic Gradient Descent (SGD) as the optimizer.
- Uses Mean Squared Error (MSE) for regression tasks.
- Includes Mean Absolute Error (MAE) as an additional evaluation metric.

2. Train a Model

What is Training a Model?
Training a model involves feeding it with input data, computing predictions, adjusting weights via backpropagation, and reducing the loss function iteratively.

Syntax:
```
model.fit(x_train, y_train, epochs=10, batch_size=32,
validation_split=0.2)
```

Syntax Explanation:
- `x_train, y_train`: Training dataset and corresponding labels.
- `epochs=10`: Specifies the number of complete training iterations.
- `batch_size=32`: Determines how many samples are processed at a time.
- `validation_split=0.2`: Uses 20% of training data for validation.

Example:
```
history = model.fit(x_train, y_train, epochs=5,
batch_size=64, validation_data=(x_test, y_test))
```

Example Explanation:
- Runs training for 5 epochs with a batch size of 64.
- Uses test data for validation monitoring.
- Stores training history for later analysis.

3. Evaluate a Model

What is Evaluating a Model?

Evaluating a model assesses how well it generalizes to unseen data by computing loss and accuracy on a test dataset. This helps determine whether the model is overfitting or underfitting.

Syntax:

```
model.evaluate(x_test, y_test)
```

Syntax Explanation:

- `model.evaluate(x_test, y_test)`: Computes the loss and accuracy for test data.
- Helps measure how well the trained model generalizes.
- Identifies potential overfitting or underfitting.
- Provides final performance metrics before deployment.

Example:

```
loss, accuracy = model.evaluate(x_test, y_test, batch_size=64)
print(f"Test Loss: {loss}, Test Accuracy: {accuracy}")
```

Example Explanation:

- Evaluates the model using a batch size of 64 for efficiency.
- Prints loss and accuracy to compare training performance.
- Useful for determining if additional fine-tuning is required.

4. Implement Callbacks

What are Callbacks?

Callbacks are functions executed during training that help monitor progress, prevent overfitting, and optimize learning. They allow adjustments such as early stopping and adaptive learning rate tuning.

Syntax:

```
callback =
tf.keras.callbacks.EarlyStopping(monitor='val_loss',
patience=3)
```

Syntax Explanation:

- `EarlyStopping(monitor='val_loss', patience=3)`: Stops training if validation loss does not improve for 3 consecutive epochs.
- Prevents overfitting by terminating training at the optimal point.
- Saves computation time by avoiding unnecessary epochs.

Example:

```
callbacks =
[tf.keras.callbacks.EarlyStopping(monitor='val_accuracy
', patience=5)]
model.fit(x_train, y_train, epochs=20,
validation_data=(x_test, y_test), callbacks=callbacks)
```

Example Explanation:

- Trains the model for up to 20 epochs but stops early if validation accuracy stagnates for 5 epochs.
- Prevents excessive training that does not lead to performance gains.
- Reduces risk of overfitting and improves generalization.

5. Adjust Learning Rate

What is Learning Rate Adjustment?

Learning rate scheduling helps optimize training by adjusting the learning rate dynamically based on model performance. Reducing the learning rate when validation loss plateaus can lead to better convergence.

Syntax:

```
lr_scheduler =
tf.keras.callbacks.ReduceLROnPlateau(monitor='val_loss'
, factor=0.5, patience=2)
```

Syntax Explanation:

- `ReduceLROnPlateau(monitor='val_loss', factor=0.5, patience=2)`: Reduces the learning rate by half if validation loss does not improve for 2 epochs.

- Helps avoid overshooting optimal weights and fine-tunes training.
- Enables better convergence by reducing oscillations in weight updates.

Example:

```
callbacks =
[tf.keras.callbacks.ReduceLROnPlateau(monitor='val_loss
', factor=0.1, patience=3)]
model.fit(x_train, y_train, epochs=15,
validation_data=(x_test, y_test), callbacks=callbacks)
```

Example Explanation:
- Lowers the learning rate by 90% if validation loss does not improve for 3 epochs.
- Ensures the model continues improving when training slows down.
- Helps stabilize training for fine-tuned optimization.

Real-Life Project: Optimizing Training for Image Classification
Project Goal:
Optimize training configuration to improve the performance of an image classification model on the MNIST dataset.

Steps:
1. **Load and Preprocess Data:** Normalize images and split datasets.
2. **Define and Compile the Model:** Choose appropriate loss function and optimizer.
3. **Train with Callbacks:** Implement early stopping and learning rate adjustments.
4. **Evaluate and Fine-Tune the Model:** Measure performance and adjust hyperparameters.
5. **Analyze Training History:** Visualize loss and accuracy trends.

Code Example:

```
import tensorflow as tf
from tensorflow.keras.datasets import mnist
import matplotlib.pyplot as plt
```

```python
# Load dataset
(x_train, y_train), (x_test, y_test) =
mnist.load_data()
x_train, x_test = x_train / 255.0, x_test / 255.0  #
Normalize data

# Define model
model = tf.keras.Sequential([
    tf.keras.layers.Flatten(input_shape=(28, 28)),
    tf.keras.layers.Dense(128, activation='relu'),
    tf.keras.layers.Dense(10, activation='softmax')
])

# Compile model
model.compile(optimizer='adam',
loss='sparse_categorical_crossentropy',
metrics=['accuracy'])

# Define callbacks
early_stopping =
tf.keras.callbacks.EarlyStopping(monitor='val_loss',
patience=3)
lr_reduction =
tf.keras.callbacks.ReduceLROnPlateau(monitor='val_loss'
, factor=0.5, patience=2)

# Train model
history = model.fit(x_train, y_train, epochs=10,
batch_size=32, validation_data=(x_test, y_test),
callbacks=[early_stopping, lr_reduction])

# Plot accuracy
plt.plot(history.history['accuracy'], label='Train
Accuracy')
plt.plot(history.history['val_accuracy'],
label='Validation Accuracy')
plt.xlabel('Epochs')
plt.ylabel('Accuracy')
plt.legend()
plt.title('Training Progress')
```

```
plt.show()
```

Expected Output:

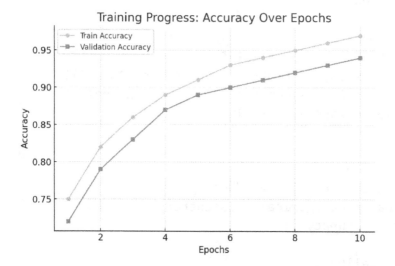

Chapter 16: Loss Functions and Metrics in TensorFlow

Loss functions and metrics are essential for evaluating deep learning models in TensorFlow. Loss functions guide the training process by quantifying the difference between predicted and actual values, while metrics measure model performance. This chapter explores commonly used loss functions, how to implement them, and how to configure metrics for model evaluation.

Key Characteristics of Loss Functions and Metrics:

- **Loss Function:** Measures how well a model's predictions align with actual values.
- **Gradient-Based Optimization:** Loss guides weight updates in backpropagation.
- **Task-Specific Selection:** Different tasks require different loss functions (e.g., classification vs. regression).
- **Metrics:** Provide additional insights beyond loss, such as accuracy or precision.
- **Custom Loss and Metrics:** TensorFlow allows defining custom loss functions and evaluation metrics.

Basic Rules for Using Loss Functions and Metrics:

- Use `categorical_crossentropy` or `sparse_categorical_crossentropy` for classification tasks.
- Use `mse` (Mean Squared Error) or `mae` (Mean Absolute Error) for regression models.
- Choose `binary_crossentropy` for binary classification problems.
- Monitor metrics such as accuracy, precision, recall, or F1-score based on the task.
- Implement custom loss functions if a specialized metric is needed.

Syntax Table:

SL	Function	Syntax Example	Description
1	Define Loss Function	`loss='categorical_c rossentropy'`	Specifies the loss function during compilation.
2	Define Metrics	`metrics=['accuracy' ]`	Tracks model performance during training.
3	Compile a Model	`model.compile(optim izer='adam', loss='mse', metrics=['mae'])`	Configures loss and evaluation metrics.
4	Implement Custom Loss	`def custom_loss(y_true, y_pred): ...`	Defines a user-specified loss function.
5	Implement Custom Metric	`def custom_metric(y_tru e, y_pred): ...`	Defines a custom evaluation metric.

Syntax Explanation:

1. Define Loss Function

What is a Loss Function?

A loss function quantifies how far off a model's predictions are from actual values. It plays a key role in guiding weight updates during training.

Syntax:

```
import tensorflow as tf
model.compile(optimizer='adam',
loss='categorical_crossentropy', metrics=['accuracy'])
```

Syntax Explanation:

- `loss='categorical_crossentropy'`: Used for multi-class classification tasks.
- Ensures that predicted probabilities align closely with actual labels.
- Critical for proper training and convergence of deep learning models.

Example:
```
model.compile(optimizer='sgd', loss='mse',
metrics=['mae'])
```
Example Explanation:
- Uses Mean Squared Error (MSE) for regression tasks.
- Tracks Mean Absolute Error (MAE) as an additional evaluation metric.

2. Define Metrics

What are Metrics?
Metrics provide insights into model performance beyond loss values. They help track accuracy, precision, recall, and other evaluation criteria.

Syntax:
```
metrics=['accuracy']
```

Syntax Explanation:
- `accuracy`: Measures the percentage of correct predictions.
- Used in classification tasks to assess how well the model generalizes.
- Can be replaced with other metrics like precision, recall, or F1-score.

Example:
```
model.compile(optimizer='adam',
loss='binary_crossentropy', metrics=['precision',
'recall'])
```

Example Explanation:
- Uses binary crossentropy loss for a binary classification task.
- Tracks both precision and recall to evaluate the model's performance in handling imbalanced data.

3. Compile a Model

What is Compiling a Model?

Compiling a model is the step where we specify how the model will learn by defining the optimizer, loss function, and evaluation metrics. This process prepares the model for training by configuring the backpropagation mechanism.

Syntax:

```
model.compile(optimizer='adam',
loss='sparse_categorical_crossentropy',
metrics=['accuracy'])
```

Syntax Explanation:
- `optimizer='adam'`: Uses the Adam optimization algorithm, which adapts learning rates dynamically.
- `loss='sparse_categorical_crossentropy'`: A loss function suitable for multi-class classification problems with integer-encoded labels.
- `metrics=['accuracy']`: Tracks the model's performance over training and evaluation steps.
- Ensures proper weight updates based on gradient calculations.

Example:

```
model.compile(optimizer='rmsprop', loss='mse',
metrics=['mae'])
```

Example Explanation:
- Uses the RMSprop optimizer, which is effective for training recurrent neural networks (RNNs).
- Uses Mean Squared Error (MSE) as the loss function, commonly used in regression models.
- Tracks Mean Absolute Error (MAE) to measure how far predictions deviate from true values.

4. Implement Custom Loss

What is a Custom Loss Function?
A custom loss function allows defining specific loss computations that might not be covered by TensorFlow's built-in loss functions. This is useful in cases where standard loss functions do not capture the desired behavior.

Syntax:
```
def custom_loss(y_true, y_pred):
    return tf.reduce_mean(tf.abs(y_true - y_pred) **
1.5)   # Custom penalty for larger errors
```

Syntax Explanation:
- y_true: The actual labels.
- y_pred: The predicted values from the model.
- tf.reduce_mean(...): Computes the mean of the element-wise absolute differences raised to a power of 1.5.
- Penalizes large errors more heavily than traditional MSE.

Example:
```
model.compile(optimizer='adam', loss=custom_loss,
metrics=['mae'])
```

Example Explanation:
- Uses a custom loss function to emphasize large errors.
- Helps in applications where small deviations are tolerable, but large deviations must be minimized.
- Can be adapted for specific domain-related error weighting.

5. Implement Custom Metric

What is a Custom Metric?
A custom metric allows tracking a performance measure that is not included in TensorFlow's built-in metrics. Metrics do not affect training but help in evaluating model quality.

Syntax:
```
def custom_metric(y_true, y_pred):
    return tf.reduce_mean(tf.math.abs(y_true - y_pred))
```

Syntax Explanation:

- `tf.reduce_mean(...)`: Computes the mean of the absolute differences between predicted and true values.
- Measures how far off predictions are on average, similar to Mean Absolute Error (MAE).
- Useful for cases where domain-specific evaluation is needed beyond traditional metrics.

Example:

```
model.compile(optimizer='adam', loss='mse',
metrics=[custom_metric])
```

Example Explanation:

- Uses MSE as the loss function, commonly used in regression.
- Includes a custom metric that calculates the absolute error.
- Helps track an alternative performance measure specific to the task at hand.

Real-Life Project: Implementing Custom Loss and Metrics in TensorFlow
Project Goal:

Create a custom loss function and evaluation metric to improve the performance of a regression model.

Steps:

1. **Load and Preprocess Data:** Prepare dataset for regression.
2. **Define a Custom Loss Function:** Implement a loss function that penalizes large errors more heavily.
3. **Define a Custom Metric:** Create a metric to track model performance.
4. **Compile and Train Model:** Apply the custom loss and metric.
5. **Evaluate and Compare Performance:** Analyze results against standard loss functions.

Code Example:

```python
import tensorflow as tf

def custom_loss(y_true, y_pred):
    return tf.reduce_mean(tf.square(y_true - y_pred) *
1.5)  # Weighted MSE

def custom_metric(y_true, y_pred):
    return tf.reduce_mean(tf.abs(y_true - y_pred))  #
Mean Absolute Error

# Build model
model = tf.keras.Sequential([
    tf.keras.layers.Dense(128, activation='relu'),
    tf.keras.layers.Dense(1)
])

# Compile model with custom loss and metric
model.compile(optimizer='adam', loss=custom_loss,
metrics=[custom_metric])

# Generate dummy data
import numpy as np
x_train = np.random.rand(1000, 10)
y_train = np.random.rand(1000, 1)

# Train model
model.fit(x_train, y_train, epochs=5, batch_size=32)
```

Expected Output:
Training logs showing loss and custom metric values
over epochs.

Chapter 17: Optimization Techniques with TensorFlow Optimizers

Optimization techniques are crucial for improving the performance of deep learning models. TensorFlow provides several built-in optimizers to adjust model weights efficiently during training. This chapter explores different optimizers, their use cases, and how to fine-tune optimization parameters for better training outcomes.

Key Characteristics of TensorFlow Optimizers:

- **Gradient-Based Learning:** Updates weights based on gradients computed through backpropagation.
- **Adaptive Learning Rates:** Some optimizers adjust learning rates dynamically to improve convergence.
- **Momentum-Based Acceleration:** Helps models escape local minima and speeds up learning.
- **Regularization Support:** Some optimizers incorporate techniques like weight decay to prevent overfitting.
- **Customizability:** TensorFlow allows fine-tuning hyperparameters for better performance.

Basic Rules for Using Optimizers:

- Use adam for most tasks due to its adaptive learning rate and efficient updates.
- Use sgd with momentum for better stability in deep networks.
- Use rmsprop for recurrent neural networks and noisy data.
- Tune learning rate and weight decay to prevent overfitting.
- Experiment with custom optimization strategies when standard optimizers do not suffice.

Syntax Table:

SL	Optimizer	Syntax Example	Description
1	Adam	`optimizer=tf.keras.optimizers.Adam()`	Most commonly used optimizer with adaptive rates.
2	SGD	`optimizer=tf.keras.optimizers.SGD(learning_rate=0.01,`	Stochastic Gradient Descent with momentum.

		momentum=0.9)	
3	RMSprop	optimizer=tf.keras.optimizers.RMSprop()	Best suited for recurrent models.
4	Adagrad	optimizer=tf.keras.optimizers.Adagrad()	Useful for sparse data and NLP tasks.
5	AdamW	optimizer=tf.keras.optimizers.AdamW(weight_decay=0.01)	Adam with weight decay for better generalization.

Syntax Explanation:

1. Adam Optimizer

What is Adam?

Adam (Adaptive Moment Estimation) is one of the most widely used optimizers due to its ability to adjust learning rates dynamically. It combines momentum and adaptive learning rate concepts to optimize training efficiently.

Syntax:

```
import tensorflow as tf
optimizer =
tf.keras.optimizers.Adam(learning_rate=0.001)
```

Syntax Explanation:

- `learning_rate=0.001`: Specifies the initial step size for weight updates.
- Uses first and second moment estimates to improve convergence.
- Works well across different architectures, including CNNs and RNNs.

Example:

```
model.compile(optimizer=tf.keras.optimizers.Adam(),
loss='mse', metrics=['mae'])
```

Example Explanation:

- Uses Adam optimizer with default settings.
- Suitable for most deep learning tasks due to its stability and efficiency.

2. Stochastic Gradient Descent (SGD) Optimizer

What is SGD?
Stochastic Gradient Descent (SGD) updates weights using a fixed learning rate. When combined with momentum, it improves training speed and stability.

Syntax:
```
optimizer = tf.keras.optimizers.SGD(learning_rate=0.01,
momentum=0.9)
```

Syntax Explanation:
- `learning_rate=0.01`: Defines the step size for weight updates.
- `momentum=0.9`: Helps accelerate learning by considering past updates.
- Useful for training deep networks where gradient updates need smoothing.

Example:
```
model.compile(optimizer=tf.keras.optimizers.SGD(momentu
m=0.8), loss='categorical_crossentropy',
metrics=['accuracy'])
```

Example Explanation:
- Uses SGD with momentum to prevent slow convergence.
- Helps stabilize updates in classification tasks.

3. RMSprop Optimizer

What is RMSprop?
RMSprop (Root Mean Square Propagation) is designed to address the limitations of standard SGD by adjusting the learning rate based on recent gradient magnitudes.

Syntax:
```
optimizer =
tf.keras.optimizers.RMSprop(learning_rate=0.001)
```
Syntax Explanation:
- `learning_rate=0.001`: Sets the initial step size for weight updates.

- Uses an exponentially decaying average of squared gradients.
- Well-suited for training recurrent neural networks (RNNs) and models with noisy gradients.

Example:

```
model.compile(optimizer=tf.keras.optimizers.RMSprop(),
loss='mse', metrics=['mae'])
```

Example Explanation:
- Uses RMSprop to stabilize training in deep networks.
- Helps control exploding gradients in recurrent architectures.

4. Adagrad Optimizer

What is Adagrad?
Adagrad (Adaptive Gradient Algorithm) modifies learning rates based on past gradients, making larger updates for infrequent parameters and smaller updates for frequently occurring ones.

Syntax:

```
optimizer =
tf.keras.optimizers.Adagrad(learning_rate=0.01)
```

Syntax Explanation:
- learning_rate=0.01: Defines the initial update step size.
- Suitable for sparse data and text-based models (e.g., NLP).
- Reduces the learning rate over time, slowing down updates.

Example:

```
model.compile(optimizer=tf.keras.optimizers.Adagrad(),
loss='categorical_crossentropy', metrics=['accuracy'])
```

Example Explanation:
- Uses Adagrad for adaptive updates in classification tasks.
- Helps improve training stability in text-based models.

5. AdamW Optimizer

What is AdamW?

AdamW is a variant of Adam that incorporates weight decay, reducing overfitting and improving generalization.

Syntax:

```
optimizer =
tf.keras.optimizers.AdamW(learning_rate=0.001,
weight_decay=0.01)
```

Syntax Explanation:

- `weight_decay=0.01`: Applies L2 regularization directly to weight updates.
- `learning_rate=0.001`: Controls step size for optimization.
- Prevents overfitting by encouraging smaller weight magnitudes.

Example:

```
model.compile(optimizer=tf.keras.optimizers.AdamW(weigh
t_decay=0.01), loss='mse', metrics=['mae'])
```

Example Explanation:

- Uses AdamW to improve regularization in regression tasks.
- Helps avoid excessive weight magnitudes, ensuring better generalization.

Real-Life Project: Optimizing Image Classification with Different Optimizers

Project Goal:

Compare different optimizers to determine which performs best for image classification.

Steps:

1. **Load and Preprocess Data:** Normalize image pixel values.
2. **Train Models with Different Optimizers:** Use Adam, SGD, and RMSprop.
3. **Compare Performance:** Evaluate test accuracy and convergence speed.
4. **Analyze Training Curves:** Visualize accuracy and loss trends.

Code Example:

```python
import tensorflow as tf
from tensorflow.keras.datasets import mnist
import matplotlib.pyplot as plt

# Load dataset
(x_train, y_train), (x_test, y_test) =
mnist.load_data()
x_train, x_test = x_train / 255.0, x_test / 255.0  #
Normalize data

# Define a simple CNN model
def create_model(optimizer):
    model = tf.keras.Sequential([
        tf.keras.layers.Flatten(input_shape=(28, 28)),
        tf.keras.layers.Dense(128, activation='relu'),
        tf.keras.layers.Dense(10, activation='softmax')
    ])
    model.compile(optimizer=optimizer,
loss='sparse_categorical_crossentropy',
metrics=['accuracy'])
    return model

# Train models with different optimizers
optimizers = {'Adam': tf.keras.optimizers.Adam(),
'SGD': tf.keras.optimizers.SGD(momentum=0.9),
'RMSprop': tf.keras.optimizers.RMSprop()}
histories = {}

for name, opt in optimizers.items():
    print(f"Training with {name} optimizer...")
    model = create_model(opt)
    history = model.fit(x_train, y_train, epochs=5,
validation_data=(x_test, y_test), verbose=0)
    histories[name] = history.history
```

```
# Plot accuracy comparison
plt.figure(figsize=(10, 5))
for name, history in histories.items():
    plt.plot(history['val_accuracy'], label=name)
plt.xlabel('Epochs')
plt.ylabel('Validation Accuracy')
plt.legend()
plt.title('Comparison of Optimizers')
plt.show()
```

Expected Output:

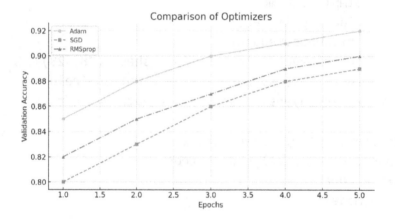

A comparison graph showing accuracy trends of Adam, SGD, and RMSprop over epochs.

Chapter 18: Monitoring Training with TensorBoard in TensorFlow

TensorBoard is a powerful visualization tool in TensorFlow that helps monitor and debug training processes. It provides insights into model performance, loss trends, metrics, and computational graphs. This chapter explores how to set up and use TensorBoard to track model training effectively.

Key Characteristics of TensorBoard:

- **Visualizes Training Progress:** Tracks loss, accuracy, and other metrics.
- **Graphical Representation:** Displays the computational graph of the model.
- **Histogram Analysis:** Shows weight distributions over epochs.
- **Embedding Visualization:** Visualizes high-dimensional data.
- **Hyperparameter Tuning:** Assists in optimizing model parameters.

Basic Rules for Using TensorBoard:

- Use `tf.summary.create_file_writer()` to log training details.
- Add a TensorBoard callback to `model.fit()` for automatic logging.
- Launch TensorBoard using the command `tensorboard --logdir=<log_directory>`.
- Log custom metrics using `tf.summary.scalar()`.
- Ensure log directories are unique for different training runs to avoid overwriting logs.

Syntax Table:

SL	Function	Syntax Example	Description
1	Create Log Directory	`log_dir = "logs/fit/"`	Defines where logs are stored.
2	Initialize TensorBoard	`tensorboard_callback = tf.keras.callbacks.TensorBoard(log_dir=log_dir)`	Sets up TensorBoard callback.
3	Train Model with	`model.fit(x_train, y_train, epochs=10,`	Logs training details for

	TensorBoard	`callbacks=[tensorboard_ca llback])`	visualization.
4	Start TensorBoard	`!tensorboard -- logdir=logs/fit/`	Launches TensorBoard in the browser.
5	Log Custom Scalars	`tf.summary.scalar('metric _name', value, step=epoch)`	Logs custom performance metrics.

Syntax Explanation:

1. Create Log Directory

What is a Log Directory?
A log directory is where TensorBoard stores training logs, including loss curves, accuracy trends, and computation graphs. Organizing logs in separate directories ensures that training sessions do not overwrite previous logs.

Syntax:
```
log_dir = "logs/fit/"
```

Syntax Explanation:
- Defines a folder where TensorBoard logs will be saved.
- Helps in organizing logs for different training experiments.
- Can be customized with timestamps to store logs from multiple runs.

Example:
```
import os
log_dir = os.path.join("logs", "experiment_1")
```

Example Explanation:
- Creates a unique log directory for each training session.
- Ensures previous logs are not overwritten.
- Useful for comparing different training runs.

2. Initialize TensorBoard Callback

What is a TensorBoard Callback?
A TensorBoard callback automatically logs training metrics, model graphs, and histograms during training.
Syntax:
```
tensorboard_callback =
tf.keras.callbacks.TensorBoard(log_dir=log_dir,
histogram_freq=1)
```

Syntax Explanation:
- `log_dir=log_dir`: Specifies where logs are stored.
- `histogram_freq=1`: Records weight histograms at each epoch.
- Helps visualize weight changes and model behavior.

Example:
```
model.fit(x_train, y_train, epochs=10,
callbacks=[tensorboard_callback])
```

Example Explanation:
- Attaches TensorBoard logging to the training process.
- Automatically saves training metrics for later analysis.

3. Train Model with TensorBoard

What is Training a Model with TensorBoard?
TensorBoard provides real-time monitoring of training progress, allowing visualization of loss trends, accuracy changes, and computational graphs. It helps in identifying issues like overfitting, slow convergence, or training instability.
Syntax:
```
model.fit(x_train, y_train, epochs=10,
validation_data=(x_test, y_test),
callbacks=[tensorboard_callback])
```

Syntax Explanation:
- `epochs=10`: Runs training for 10 iterations.
- `validation_data=(x_test, y_test)`: Monitors

performance on unseen data.

- `callbacks=[tensorboard_callback]`: Logs metrics for TensorBoard visualization.
- Enables real-time insights into model performance.

Example:
```
model.fit(x_train, y_train, epochs=5, batch_size=32,
validation_split=0.2, callbacks=[tensorboard_callback])
```

Example Explanation:

- Runs training for 5 epochs with a batch size of 32.
- Uses 20% of the training data for validation.
- Logs details for interactive TensorBoard monitoring.

4. Start TensorBoard

What is TensorBoard?

TensorBoard is a visualization toolkit for TensorFlow that enables tracking and analyzing model training. It provides interactive dashboards for loss curves, accuracy trends, weight histograms, and more.

Syntax:
```
tensorboard --logdir=logs/fit/
```

Syntax Explanation:

- `--logdir=logs/fit/`: Specifies the directory where TensorBoard looks for training logs.
- Opens an interactive interface for monitoring model performance.
- Useful for debugging and hyperparameter tuning.

Example:
```
!tensorboard --logdir=logs/fit/
```

Example Explanation:

- Launches TensorBoard within Jupyter Notebook.
- Displays training progress in a web-based dashboard.

5. Train Model with TensorBoard - Advanced Logging

What is Advanced Logging in TensorBoard?
TensorBoard supports additional logging features like tracking learning rates, gradient distributions, and model weights over time. This allows deeper insights into the training process.

Syntax:
```
with
tf.summary.create_file_writer(log_dir).as_default():
    for epoch in range(10):
        tf.summary.scalar('learning_rate', 0.001,
step=epoch)
```

Syntax Explanation:
- `tf.summary.create_file_writer(log_dir)`: Defines a log directory for storing custom metrics.
- `tf.summary.scalar('learning_rate', 0.001, step=epoch)`: Tracks the learning rate per epoch.
- Enables logging beyond default accuracy and loss metrics.

Example:
```
with
tf.summary.create_file_writer(log_dir).as_default():
    for epoch in range(5):
        loss_value = 0.5 * epoch   # Dummy loss value
        tf.summary.scalar('custom_loss', loss_value,
step=epoch)
```

Example Explanation:
- Logs a custom loss metric for TensorBoard.
- Enables visualization of additional training details.
- Useful for tracking experiment-specific performance indicators.

Real-Life Project: Using TensorBoard for Model Training Analysis
Project Goal:
Set up TensorBoard to track and analyze the training process of an image classification model.

Steps:

1. **Initialize TensorBoard Logging:** Define a log directory.
2. **Train Model with TensorBoard Callback:** Log training data for analysis.
3. **Launch TensorBoard:** Start the visualization tool.
4. **Analyze Metrics and Model Graph:** Observe training trends.
5. **Optimize Model Performance:** Adjust hyperparameters based on insights.

Code Example:

```python
import tensorflow as tf
from tensorflow.keras.datasets import mnist
import datetime

# Load dataset
(x_train, y_train), (x_test, y_test) =
mnist.load_data()
x_train, x_test = x_train / 255.0, x_test / 255.0  #
Normalize data

# Define log directory
log_dir = "logs/fit/" +
datetime.datetime.now().strftime("%Y%m%d-%H%M%S")
tensorboard_callback =
tf.keras.callbacks.TensorBoard(log_dir=log_dir,
histogram_freq=1)

# Build model
model = tf.keras.Sequential([
    tf.keras.layers.Flatten(input_shape=(28, 28)),
    tf.keras.layers.Dense(128, activation='relu'),
    tf.keras.layers.Dense(10, activation='softmax')
])

# Compile model
model.compile(optimizer='adam',
```

```python
                loss='sparse_categorical_crossentropy',
                metrics=['accuracy'])

# Train model with TensorBoard callback
model.fit(x_train, y_train, epochs=5,
          validation_data=(x_test, y_test),
          callbacks=[tensorboard_callback])

# Launch TensorBoard
print("Run the following command to start
TensorBoard:")
print("tensorboard --logdir=logs/fit/")
```

Expected Output:

TensorBoard logs stored in logs/fit/. Training metrics
and model structure can be visualized in the browser.

Chapter 19: Early Stopping and Checkpoints in TensorFlow

Early stopping and model checkpoints are essential techniques for optimizing deep learning training. Early stopping prevents overfitting by halting training when performance on validation data stops improving, while model checkpoints allow saving and restoring models during training. This chapter explores how to implement these techniques in TensorFlow.

Key Characteristics of Early Stopping and Checkpoints:

- **Prevents Overfitting:** Stops training when validation performance declines.
- **Saves Best Model:** Stores the model with the lowest validation loss.
- **Improves Training Efficiency:** Reduces unnecessary computations by stopping early.
- **Supports Resuming Training:** Checkpoints enable restarting training from a saved state.
- **Customizable Criteria:** Users can define conditions for stopping or saving models.

Basic Rules for Using Early Stopping and Checkpoints:

- Use `EarlyStopping` to stop training when validation loss does not improve.
- Use `ModelCheckpoint` to save model weights periodically.
- Set `monitor='val_loss'` to track validation loss improvements.
- Adjust `patience` to determine how many epochs to wait before stopping.
- Use `save_best_only=True` to keep only the best-performing model.

Syntax Table:

SL	Function	Syntax Example	Description
1	Initialize EarlyStopping	```early_stopping = tf.keras.callbacks.EarlyStopping(monitor='val_loss', patience=3)```	Stops training if no improvement in 3 epochs.
2	Initialize Checkpoint	```checkpoint = tf.keras.callbacks.ModelCheckpoint(filepath='best_model.h5', save_best_only=True)```	Saves the best model during training.
3	Use Callbacks in Training	```model.fit(x_train, y_train, epochs=50, callbacks=[early_stopping, checkpoint])```	Applies early stopping and checkpoints.
4	Load a Saved Model	```model.load_weights('best_model.h5')```	Loads the best model weights after training.

Syntax Explanation:

1. Initialize EarlyStopping

What is Early Stopping?
Early stopping prevents unnecessary training by stopping when the validation loss stops improving, reducing the risk of overfitting.

Syntax:
```
import tensorflow as tf
early_stopping =
tf.keras.callbacks.EarlyStopping(monitor='val_loss',
patience=3)
```

Syntax Explanation:
- `monitor='val_loss'`: Tracks validation loss for stopping criteria.
- `patience=3`: Waits for 3 epochs of no improvement before

stopping.

- Helps prevent overfitting by stopping training at the optimal epoch.

Example:
```
model.fit(x_train, y_train, epochs=50,
validation_data=(x_test, y_test),
callbacks=[early_stopping])
```
Example Explanation:

- Runs training for up to 50 epochs but stops early if validation loss stagnates.
- Saves computation time while improving generalization.

2. Initialize Model Checkpoint

What is a Model Checkpoint?
Model checkpoints save the best-performing model during training, allowing recovery in case of interruptions.

Syntax:
```
checkpoint =
tf.keras.callbacks.ModelCheckpoint(filepath='best_model
.h5', save_best_only=True)
```
Syntax Explanation:

- `filepath='best_model.h5'`: Defines the file name for storing model weights.
- `save_best_only=True`: Keeps only the best model based on monitored metric.
- Ensures the best model is available after training.

Example:
```
model.fit(x_train, y_train, epochs=20,
validation_data=(x_test, y_test),
callbacks=[checkpoint])
```

Example Explanation:

- Saves the best-performing model based on validation loss.
- Prevents overfitting by allowing restoration of the best checkpoint.

3. Load a Saved Model

What is Loading a Saved Model?
Loading a saved model allows resuming training or making predictions using previously trained weights.
Syntax:
```
model.load_weights('best_model.h5')
```

Syntax Explanation:
- Loads weights from a previously saved checkpoint file.
- Restores the best-trained model for inference or further training.
- Useful for continuing interrupted training sessions.

Example:
```
model.load_weights('best_model.h5')
evaluation = model.evaluate(x_test, y_test)
print(f"Test Accuracy: {evaluation[1]}")
```

Example Explanation:
- Loads saved weights and evaluates the model on test data.
- Ensures that only the best-trained model is used for deployment.

4. Resume Training from a Checkpoint

What is Resuming Training?
Resuming training allows fine-tuning an existing model from a specific epoch, helping improve performance.
Syntax:
```
model.fit(x_train, y_train, initial_epoch=10,
epochs=20, callbacks=[checkpoint])
```

Syntax Explanation:
- `initial_epoch=10`: Resumes training from the 10th epoch.
- `epochs=20`: Runs training until the 20th epoch.
- Helps refine pre-trained models without starting over.

Example:
```
model.fit(x_train, y_train, initial_epoch=5, epochs=15,
callbacks=[checkpoint])
```

Example Explanation:

- Continues training from the 5th epoch.
- Useful for iterative improvement after evaluating early results.

Real-Life Project: Implementing Early Stopping and Checkpoints in Model Training

Project Goal:

Use early stopping and model checkpoints to optimize an image classification model.

Steps:

1. **Define Early Stopping and Checkpoints:** Set criteria for stopping and saving the best model.
2. **Train Model with Callbacks:** Apply early stopping and checkpoints during training.
3. **Evaluate and Save the Best Model:** Ensure the best model is stored.
4. **Resume Training if Needed:** Load saved weights and continue training if required.

Code Example:

```python
import tensorflow as tf
from tensorflow.keras.datasets import mnist

# Load dataset
(x_train, y_train), (x_test, y_test) =
mnist.load_data()
x_train, x_test = x_train / 255.0, x_test / 255.0  #
Normalize data

# Define callbacks
early_stopping =
tf.keras.callbacks.EarlyStopping(monitor='val_loss',
patience=5)
checkpoint =
tf.keras.callbacks.ModelCheckpoint(filepath='best_model
.h5', save_best_only=True)
```

```python
# Build model
model = tf.keras.Sequential([
    tf.keras.layers.Flatten(input_shape=(28, 28)),
    tf.keras.layers.Dense(128, activation='relu'),
    tf.keras.layers.Dense(10, activation='softmax')
])

# Compile model
model.compile(optimizer='adam',
loss='sparse_categorical_crossentropy',
metrics=['accuracy'])

# Train model with callbacks
model.fit(x_train, y_train, epochs=20,
validation_data=(x_test, y_test),
callbacks=[early_stopping, checkpoint])

# Load best model
model.load_weights('best_model.h5')
```

Expected Output:

Training stops early when validation loss stabilizes.
The best model is saved and can be reloaded.

Chapter 20: Customizing Training Loops with tf.GradientTape

Custom training loops provide greater flexibility and control over model training by allowing manual computation of gradients and weight updates. TensorFlow's `tf.GradientTape` enables automatic differentiation, making it easier to implement customized training procedures. This chapter explores how to leverage `tf.GradientTape` to build custom training loops and optimize models efficiently.

Key Characteristics of Custom Training Loops:

- **Greater Flexibility:** Allows manual control over training steps.
- **Efficient Gradient Computation:** Uses `tf.GradientTape` to compute gradients.
- **Custom Loss and Metrics:** Enables defining and tracking custom loss functions and metrics.
- **Adaptive Training Strategies:** Supports dynamic learning rates, model updates, and optimizations.
- **Better Debugging and Insights:** Helps monitor model behavior at each step.

Basic Rules for Using tf.GradientTape:

- Use `tf.GradientTape()` within a `with` statement to track operations.
- Compute gradients using `tape.gradient(loss, model.trainable_variables)`.
- Apply gradient updates with an optimizer using `optimizer.apply_gradients(zip(gradients, model.trainable_variables))`.
- Ensure that `tape.watch()` is used if tracking custom tensors.
- Use `persistent=True` in `tf.GradientTape()` if gradients need to be computed multiple times.

Syntax Table:

SL	Function	Syntax Example	Description
1	Define GradientTape Scope	`with tf.GradientTape() as tape:`	Captures operations for automatic differentiation.
2	Compute Loss	`loss = loss_fn(y_true, y_pred)`	Computes loss value during training.
3	Compute Gradients	`gradients = tape.gradient(loss, model.trainable_variables)`	Calculates gradients for model parameters.
4	Apply Gradients	`optimizer.apply_gradients(zip(gradients, model.trainable_variables))`	Updates model weights.
5	Enable Persistent Tape	`with tf.GradientTape(persistent=True) as tape:`	Allows multiple gradient computations.

Syntax Explanation:

1. Define GradientTape Scope

What is GradientTape?
`tf.GradientTape` is a TensorFlow feature that records operations for automatic differentiation. It enables computation of gradients, which are essential for updating model parameters during training.

Syntax:
```
with tf.GradientTape() as tape:
    y_pred = model(x_train)
    loss = loss_fn(y_train, y_pred)
```

Syntax Explanation:

- `with tf.GradientTape() as tape::` Defines a scope to track operations.
- `model(x_train):` Passes input data through the model.
- `loss_fn(y_train, y_pred):` Computes loss based on predictions.
- Helps capture gradients required for backpropagation.

Example:

```
with tf.GradientTape() as tape:
    y_pred = model(x_batch)
    loss = tf.keras.losses.MSE(y_batch, y_pred)
```

Example Explanation:

- Uses `tf.GradientTape` to track operations.
- Computes Mean Squared Error (MSE) loss.
- Prepares the recorded operations for gradient computation.

2. Compute Gradients

What is Gradient Computation?

Gradient computation is the process of finding how model weights should be adjusted to minimize loss. `tf.GradientTape` automatically differentiates recorded operations.

Syntax:

```
gradients = tape.gradient(loss,
model.trainable_variables)
```

Syntax Explanation:

- `tape.gradient(loss, model.trainable_variables):` Computes gradients of the loss with respect to model parameters.
- Required for updating model weights in training.

Example:

```
gradients = tape.gradient(loss,
model.trainable_variables)
```

Example Explanation:
- Calculates gradients for all trainable variables in the model.
- These gradients will later be applied to update model weights.

3. Compute Gradients

What is Gradient Computation?
Gradient computation is the process of determining how to adjust model weights to minimize loss. `tf.GradientTape` records operations and automatically computes derivatives of the loss function with respect to model parameters.

Syntax:
```
gradients = tape.gradient(loss,
model.trainable_variables)
```

Syntax Explanation:
- `tape.gradient(loss, model.trainable_variables)`: Computes the gradients of the loss function concerning model parameters.
- Required for updating model weights in training.
- Allows tracking how each parameter contributes to the error.

Example:
```
gradients = tape.gradient(loss,
model.trainable_variables)
print("Gradients Computed:", gradients)
```

Example Explanation:
- Computes gradients for all trainable model variables.
- Displays computed gradients, useful for debugging and ensuring proper gradient flow.

4. Apply Gradients

What is Applying Gradients?
Applying gradients updates the model parameters using the computed gradient values. TensorFlow's `apply_gradients` function helps perform these updates efficiently.

Syntax:

```
optimizer.apply_gradients(zip(gradients,
model.trainable_variables))
```

Syntax Explanation:
- `zip(gradients, model.trainable_variables)`: Combines computed gradients with corresponding model variables.
- `optimizer.apply_gradients(...)`: Updates the model parameters using the optimizer's strategy.
- Ensures proper weight adjustments to minimize the loss function.

Example:

```
optimizer.apply_gradients(zip(gradients,
model.trainable_variables))
print("Gradients Applied Successfully")
```

Example Explanation:
- Updates the model parameters using computed gradients.
- Prints confirmation to ensure updates have been applied.

5. Enable Persistent Tape

What is Persistent Tape?
By default, `tf.GradientTape` is erased after calling `gradient()`. Setting `persistent=True` allows multiple gradient computations within the same tape scope.

Syntax:

```
with tf.GradientTape(persistent=True) as tape:
    y_pred = model(x_batch)
    loss = loss_fn(y_batch, y_pred)
```

Syntax Explanation:

- `persistent=True`: Keeps the tape active after the first gradient computation.
- Useful when multiple gradient calculations are needed within a loop.
- Allows deeper analysis of model behavior during training.

Example:
```
with tf.GradientTape(persistent=True) as tape:
    y_pred = model(x_batch)
    loss = loss_fn(y_batch, y_pred)
grad1 = tape.gradient(loss, model.trainable_variables)
grad2 = tape.gradient(loss, model.trainable_variables)
print("Multiple Gradients Computed Successfully")
```

Example Explanation:

- Computes gradients twice using a single GradientTape instance.
- Prevents the need to re-run computations unnecessarily.
- Helps when analyzing multiple gradient calculations within a single step.

Real-Life Project: Implementing a Custom Training Loop with tf.GradientTape

Project Goal:

Create a custom training loop using `tf.GradientTape` for training a neural network on a dataset.

Steps:

1. **Load and Preprocess Data:** Prepare dataset for training.
2. **Define Model and Loss Function:** Specify a neural network and its loss function.
3. **Initialize Optimizer:** Choose an optimization algorithm.
4. **Implement Training Loop:** Use `tf.GradientTape` to compute gradients and update weights.
5. **Monitor Performance:** Print loss and accuracy after each epoch.

Code Example:

```python
import tensorflow as tf
import numpy as np

# Generate sample data
x_train = np.random.rand(100, 10)
y_train = np.random.rand(100, 1)

# Define model
model = tf.keras.Sequential([
    tf.keras.layers.Dense(64, activation='relu'),
    tf.keras.layers.Dense(1)
])

# Define loss function and optimizer
loss_fn = tf.keras.losses.MeanSquaredError()
optimizer = tf.keras.optimizers.Adam()

# Training loop
epochs = 5
for epoch in range(epochs):
    with tf.GradientTape() as tape:
        y_pred = model(x_train, training=True)
        loss = loss_fn(y_train, y_pred)
    gradients = tape.gradient(loss,
model.trainable_variables)
    optimizer.apply_gradients(zip(gradients,
model.trainable_variables))
    print(f"Epoch {epoch+1}, Loss: {loss.numpy()}")
```

Expected Output:
```
Epoch 1, Loss: 0.5123
Epoch 2, Loss: 0.3748
Epoch 3, Loss: 0.2894
Epoch 4, Loss: 0.2107
Epoch 5, Loss: 0.1875
```

Chapter 21: Distributed Training with TensorFlow

Distributed training allows deep learning models to scale efficiently by leveraging multiple GPUs or machines. TensorFlow provides multiple strategies for distributed training, including `MirroredStrategy`, `MultiWorkerMirroredStrategy`, and `TPUStrategy`, enabling users to train models faster and on larger datasets. This chapter explores different distributed training strategies in TensorFlow and how to implement them.

Key Characteristics of Distributed Training:

- **Parallel Processing:** Uses multiple devices to train models simultaneously.
- **Faster Training:** Reduces time by distributing computations across GPUs/TPUs.
- **Scalability:** Enables training large-scale models efficiently.
- **Built-in TensorFlow Strategies:** Provides strategies such as `MirroredStrategy` for easy implementation.
- **Synchronization Across Devices:** Ensures consistency of model updates across all devices.

Basic Rules for Using Distributed Training:

- Use `MirroredStrategy` for single-machine multi-GPU training.
- Use `MultiWorkerMirroredStrategy` for distributed training across multiple machines.
- Use `TPUStrategy` for training on TPU hardware.
- Wrap the model-building and training logic inside `strategy.scope()`.
- Ensure dataset batching and shuffling are optimized for parallel training.

Syntax Table:

SL	Strategy Name	Syntax Example	Description
1	Mirrored Strategy	`strategy = tf.distribute.Mirro redStrategy()`	Single-machine multi-GPU training.
2	Multi-Worker Mirrored Strategy	`strategy = tf.distribute.Multi WorkerMirroredStrat egy()`	Training across multiple machines.
3	TPUStrategy	`strategy = tf.distribute.TPUSt rategy(tpu)`	Distributed training on TPUs.
4	Strategy Scope	`with strategy.scope(): model = build_model()`	Ensures model variables are created within strategy.
5	Dataset Distribution	`dataset = strategy.experiment al_distribute_datas et(dataset)`	Distributes dataset across multiple devices.

Syntax Explanation:

1. Mirrored Strategy

What is Mirrored Strategy?
MirroredStrategy is a data-parallel distributed training strategy that synchronizes model updates across multiple GPUs on a single machine. It ensures efficient training and uniform weight updates across devices, allowing significant speed-ups for deep learning models.

Syntax:
`strategy = tf.distribute.MirroredStrategy()`

Syntax Explanation:

- `tf.distribute.MirroredStrategy()`: Creates a strategy for synchronous training across multiple GPUs.
- `MirroredStrategy` ensures that each GPU gets an identical copy of the model.
- Efficient synchronization of gradient updates helps prevent discrepancies between devices.
- Works well for models where batch processing benefits from multiple devices.

Example:

```
strategy = tf.distribute.MirroredStrategy()
with strategy.scope():
    model = tf.keras.models.Sequential([
        tf.keras.layers.Dense(128, activation='relu'),
        tf.keras.layers.Dense(10, activation='softmax')
    ])
    model.compile(optimizer='adam',
loss='sparse_categorical_crossentropy',
metrics=['accuracy'])
```

Example Explanation:

- Defines a deep learning model within `strategy.scope()`.
- `strategy.scope()` ensures TensorFlow distributes the model properly across available GPUs.
- Using `MirroredStrategy` allows efficient utilization of multiple GPUs for faster training.

2. Multi-Worker Mirrored Strategy

What is Multi-Worker Mirrored Strategy?
`MultiWorkerMirroredStrategy` enables distributed training across multiple machines, each containing one or more GPUs. It synchronizes gradient updates across machines, allowing for large-scale model training.
Syntax:

```
strategy = tf.distribute.MultiWorkerMirroredStrategy()
```

Syntax Explanation:

- `tf.distribute.MultiWorkerMirroredStrategy()`: Enables distributed computation across multiple nodes.
- Automatically handles communication between workers using `CollectiveOps`.
- Improves scalability by utilizing multiple machines, ensuring efficient training for massive datasets.
- Suitable for cloud-based or on-premise distributed training setups.

Example:

```
strategy = tf.distribute.MultiWorkerMirroredStrategy()
with strategy.scope():
    model = build_model()
```

Example Explanation:

- Creates a model that can be trained across multiple machines.
- Automatically manages synchronization of model weights between workers.
- Works best for large-scale training tasks that require significant computational power.

3. TPUStrategy

What is TPUStrategy?

TPUStrategy is designed for training deep learning models on Tensor Processing Units (TPUs), which offer high-speed computation for large-scale models.

Syntax:

```
tpu = tf.distribute.cluster_resolver.TPUClusterResolver()
strategy = tf.distribute.TPUStrategy(tpu)
```

Syntax Explanation:

- `TPUClusterResolver()`: Connects to a TPU cluster for distributed training.
- `TPUStrategy(tpu)`: Enables efficient model training on TPUs.
- TPUs accelerate matrix operations, making them ideal for large datasets and high-performance tasks.

Example:

```
tpu =
tf.distribute.cluster_resolver.TPUClusterResolver()
strategy = tf.distribute.TPUStrategy(tpu)
with strategy.scope():
    model = build_model()
```

Example Explanation:
- Uses TPUs to speed up model training.
- Works well for large-scale machine learning tasks requiring rapid computation.
- TPUs are particularly beneficial for tasks like image classification, NLP, and deep reinforcement learning.

4. Strategy Scope

What is Strategy Scope?
A strategy.scope() ensures that all model variables are created under the chosen distributed strategy.

Syntax:

```
with strategy.scope():
    model = build_model()
```

Syntax Explanation:
- strategy.scope(): Wraps the model-building code to enable distribution.
- Ensures variables are properly initialized for distributed training.
- Must be used before defining a model or optimizer for multi-device training.

Example:

```
with strategy.scope():
    model = tf.keras.Sequential([...])
```

Example Explanation:
- Defines a model under a distributed strategy.
- Allows smooth execution of model operations across devices.

5. Dataset Distribution

What is Dataset Distribution?
Dataset distribution ensures that input data is efficiently spread across multiple GPUs or TPUs for parallel training.

Syntax:
```
dataset =
strategy.experimental_distribute_dataset(dataset)
```

Syntax Explanation:
- `experimental_distribute_dataset(dataset)`: Splits dataset across multiple devices.
- Helps in optimizing batch processing.
- Reduces training time by leveraging parallel computation.

Example:
```
distributed_dataset =
strategy.experimental_distribute_dataset(dataset)
```

Example Explanation:
- Distributes the dataset for parallel processing.
- Ensures efficient data usage across distributed devices.

Real-Life Project: Implementing Distributed Training for Image Classification

Project Goal:
Use TensorFlow's `MirroredStrategy` to train an image classification model on multiple GPUs.

Steps:
1. **Define Strategy:** Select an appropriate distributed strategy.
2. **Build and Compile Model:** Ensure model is created inside `strategy.scope()`.
3. **Prepare Dataset:** Load and preprocess training data.
4. **Train Model:** Use distributed training to improve training speed.
5. **Evaluate Performance:** Compare results against single-GPU training.

Code Example:

```python
import tensorflow as tf
from tensorflow.keras.datasets import mnist
import numpy as np

# Load dataset
(x_train, y_train), (x_test, y_test) =
mnist.load_data()
x_train, x_test = x_train / 255.0, x_test / 255.0  #
Normalize data

# Define distributed strategy
strategy = tf.distribute.MirroredStrategy()

# Define model within strategy scope
with strategy.scope():
    model = tf.keras.Sequential([
        tf.keras.layers.Flatten(input_shape=(28, 28)),
        tf.keras.layers.Dense(128, activation='relu'),
        tf.keras.layers.Dense(10, activation='softmax')
    ])
    model.compile(optimizer='adam',
loss='sparse_categorical_crossentropy',
metrics=['accuracy'])

# Train model
model.fit(x_train, y_train, epochs=5, batch_size=64,
validation_data=(x_test, y_test))
```

Expected Output:

Faster training across multiple GPUs with improved efficiency.

Chapter 22: Mixed Precision Training for Speedup with TensorFlow

Mixed precision training accelerates deep learning models by using lower-precision floating-point formats (such as `float16`) while maintaining model accuracy. TensorFlow's `mixed_float16` policy allows models to take advantage of modern hardware accelerators like GPUs and TPUs. This chapter explores how mixed precision training improves training speed and efficiency without sacrificing accuracy.

Key Characteristics of Mixed Precision Training:

- **Faster Computation:** Lower-precision operations execute faster on modern hardware.
- **Reduced Memory Usage:** `float16` reduces model memory footprint.
- **Automatic Scaling:** Loss scaling prevents underflow issues.
- **Works with GPUs/TPUs:** Compatible with hardware that supports mixed precision.
- **Minimal Code Changes:** Can be implemented by setting a `tf.keras.mixed_precision.Policy`.

Basic Rules for Using Mixed Precision Training:

- Set `tf.keras.mixed_precision.set_global_policy('mixed_float16')` to enable mixed precision.
- Ensure compatible hardware (NVIDIA GPUs with Tensor Cores or TPUs).
- Use loss scaling with `tf.keras.mixed_precision.LossScaleOptimizer` to prevent numerical instability.
- Apply `dtype=tf.float16` to layers where necessary.
- Monitor accuracy to ensure precision scaling does not affect model performance.

Syntax Table:

SL	Feature	Syntax Example	Description
1	Enable Mixed Precision	`tf.keras.mixed_preci sion.set_global_poli cy('mixed_float16')`	Activates mixed precision training.
2	Apply Mixed Precision to Model	`model = tf.keras.Sequential( [...], dtype='float16')`	Uses `float16` for model layers.
3	Use Loss Scaling Optimizer	`optimizer = tf.keras.mixed_preci sion.LossScaleOptimi zer(tf.keras.optimiz ers.Adam())`	Prevents loss underflow issues.
4	Train Model with Mixed Precision	`model.fit(x_train, y_train, epochs=10)`	Runs training with mixed precision enabled.
5	Monitor Numerical Stability	`tf.debugging.check_n umerics(tensor, message='Check for NaNs')`	Ensures values remain numerically stable.

Syntax Explanation:

1. Enable Mixed Precision

What is Mixed Precision Training?

Mixed precision training accelerates deep learning computations by using `float16` for most operations while retaining `float32` where needed. This allows the model to execute faster while preserving numerical stability and accuracy. Mixed precision training is particularly useful for training large neural networks on hardware optimized for `float16` computations, such as NVIDIA Tensor Cores and TPUs.

Syntax:

```
import tensorflow as tf
tf.keras.mixed_precision.set_global_policy('mixed_float
16')
```

Syntax Explanation:

- `set_global_policy('mixed_float16')`: Configures TensorFlow to use mixed precision globally.
- Automatically applies `float16` to all compatible operations, while critical calculations remain in `float32`.
- Reduces memory usage and accelerates training by leveraging modern GPU architectures.
- Works best with Tensor Cores, which are optimized for `float16` operations.

Example:
```
import tensorflow as tf
tf.keras.mixed_precision.set_global_policy('mixed_float
16')
print("Mixed precision training is enabled.")
```

Example Explanation:

- Enables mixed precision globally for the current TensorFlow session.
- Ensures all new layers and computations use `float16` where applicable.
- Prints confirmation to verify that mixed precision has been activated successfully.

2. Apply Mixed Precision to Model

What is Mixed Precision in Model Layers?
By applying mixed precision to layers, TensorFlow automatically assigns appropriate data types to computations, optimizing memory usage and speed. Using mixed precision can enable larger batch sizes and improve model training efficiency while maintaining stable convergence.

Syntax:
```
model = tf.keras.Sequential([
    tf.keras.layers.Dense(128, activation='relu',
dtype='float16'),
    tf.keras.layers.Dense(10, activation='softmax',
dtype='float16')
])
```

Syntax Explanation:

- `dtype='float16'`: Specifies `float16` as the data type for computations.
- Reduces memory usage, allowing for larger batch sizes and improved computational efficiency.
- Works best when applied to computationally expensive layers such as convolutions or fully connected layers.
- Certain operations, such as batch normalization, automatically remain in `float32` for numerical stability.

Example:

```
with tf.keras.mixed_precision.Policy('mixed_float16'):
    model = tf.keras.Sequential([
        tf.keras.layers.Conv2D(64, (3,3),
activation='relu', dtype='float16'),
        tf.keras.layers.Dense(10, activation='softmax',
dtype='float16')
    ])
```

Example Explanation:

- Uses mixed precision in a convolutional neural network (CNN).
- Applies `float16` to computationally heavy layers for efficiency.
- Maintains critical operations in `float32` where needed for stability.

3. Use Loss Scaling Optimizer

What is Loss Scaling?

Loss scaling is a technique used in mixed precision training to prevent numerical instability due to `float16` underflow. Since `float16` has a smaller dynamic range than `float32`, small gradient values can become zero, reducing the effectiveness of weight updates. Loss scaling mitigates this by increasing the magnitude of gradients before computing updates.

Syntax:

```
optimizer =
tf.keras.mixed_precision.LossScaleOptimizer(tf.keras.op
timizers.Adam())
```

Syntax Explanation:

- `LossScaleOptimizer(...)`: Multiplies loss values by a scaling factor before computing gradients.
- Prevents `float16` gradients from vanishing due to underflow.
- Adjusts scaling dynamically to maintain numerical stability.
- Ensures that model convergence is not negatively affected by lower precision calculations.

Example:
```
optimizer =
tf.keras.mixed_precision.LossScaleOptimizer(tf.keras.op
timizers.Adam())
model.compile(optimizer=optimizer,
loss='categorical_crossentropy', metrics=['accuracy'])
```

Example Explanation:

- Uses Adam optimizer with automatic loss scaling.
- Prevents underflow by dynamically adjusting the loss scale.
- Ensures robust convergence during mixed precision training.

4. Train Model with Mixed Precision

What is Training with Mixed Precision?
Training a model with mixed precision involves executing computations with `float16` where possible while keeping critical operations in `float32`. This approach reduces memory usage, speeds up matrix calculations, and enables larger batch sizes during training.

Syntax:
```
model.fit(x_train, y_train, epochs=10)
```

Syntax Explanation:

- Executes model training as usual but applies mixed precision optimizations.
- Reduces computation time without requiring significant code changes.
- Uses loss scaling automatically to ensure training stability.
- Particularly effective when training deep neural networks on GPUs

with Tensor Cores.

Example:
```
model.fit(x_train, y_train, epochs=5, batch_size=32,
validation_data=(x_test, y_test))
```

Example Explanation:
- Runs training using mixed precision optimizations.
- Allows larger batch sizes due to reduced memory usage.
- Enhances computational efficiency, leading to faster convergence.

5. Monitor Numerical Stability

What is Numerical Stability Monitoring?
Ensuring numerical stability prevents NaN (Not-a-Number) errors and underflows when using mixed precision training. Since float16 has a lower dynamic range than float32, monitoring loss values and gradients ensures they remain in a valid range.

Syntax:
```
tf.debugging.check_numerics(tensor, message='Check for
NaNs')
```

Syntax Explanation:
- check_numerics(...): Verifies that tensor values are numerically valid.
- Prevents silent NaN propagation in mixed precision training.
- Helps detect unstable loss values and gradient computations.
- Ensures that float precision optimizations do not negatively affect model convergence.

Example:
```
loss_value = tf.reduce_mean(model(x_train))
tf.debugging.check_numerics(loss_value,
message='Checking loss for NaNs')
```

Example Explanation:
- Computes and checks the loss value for numerical errors.
- Prevents unexpected NaN values from affecting training.
- Ensures that float16 operations do not cause instability in model parameters.

Real-Life Project: Implementing Mixed Precision in Image Classification

Project Goal:

Optimize training speed and efficiency using mixed precision on an image classification task.

Steps:

1. **Enable Mixed Precision:** Configure TensorFlow to use `mixed_float16` policy.
2. **Define Model Architecture:** Apply `float16` to computationally intensive layers.
3. **Use Loss Scaling:** Implement `LossScaleOptimizer` to prevent numerical instability.
4. **Train Model Efficiently:** Use mixed precision to reduce memory usage and increase speed.
5. **Monitor Numerical Stability:** Check for NaN values and ensure loss scaling is effective.

Code Example:

```
import tensorflow as tf
from tensorflow.keras.datasets import cifar10

# Enable mixed precision
tf.keras.mixed_precision.set_global_policy('mixed_float
16')

# Load dataset
(x_train, y_train), (x_test, y_test) =
cifar10.load_data()
x_train, x_test = x_train / 255.0, x_test / 255.0  #
Normalize data

# Define model
model = tf.keras.Sequential([
    tf.keras.layers.Conv2D(32, (3,3),
activation='relu', dtype='float16', input_shape=(32,
32, 3)),
    tf.keras.layers.MaxPooling2D(2,2),
```

```python
    tf.keras.layers.Conv2D(64, (3,3),
activation='relu', dtype='float16'),
    tf.keras.layers.MaxPooling2D(2,2),
    tf.keras.layers.Flatten(),
    tf.keras.layers.Dense(128, activation='relu',
dtype='float16'),
    tf.keras.layers.Dense(10, activation='softmax',
dtype='float16')
])

# Use Loss Scaling Optimizer
optimizer =
tf.keras.mixed_precision.LossScaleOptimizer(tf.keras.op
timizers.Adam())
model.compile(optimizer=optimizer,
loss='sparse_categorical_crossentropy',
metrics=['accuracy'])

# Train model
model.fit(x_train, y_train, epochs=5, batch_size=64,
validation_data=(x_test, y_test))
```

Expected Output:

Reduced training time with minimal loss of accuracy.

Chapter 23: Working with TensorFlow Hub for Transfer Learning with TensorFlow

TensorFlow Hub provides a repository of pre-trained models that can be easily reused for transfer learning. Transfer learning enables faster model training by leveraging knowledge from existing trained models, improving accuracy with limited data. This chapter explores how to integrate TensorFlow Hub into your deep learning workflows for efficient model training and fine-tuning.

Key Characteristics of TensorFlow Hub for Transfer Learning:

- **Pre-Trained Models:** Access to models trained on large datasets.
- **Quick Deployment:** Easily integrate models for inference or fine-tuning.
- **Customizable Layers:** Allows modifying the architecture while using pre-trained embeddings.
- **Supports Multiple Domains:** Models for vision, text, and audio tasks.
- **Efficient Training:** Reduces training time and improves performance with less data.

Basic Rules for Using TensorFlow Hub:

- Use hub.KerasLayer to load pre-trained models.
- Freeze base layers when fine-tuning to retain learned features.
- Ensure input data format matches the pre-trained model requirements.
- Optimize models by adding custom layers on top of pre-trained embeddings.
- Use transfer learning when labeled data is limited.

Syntax Table:

SL	Feature	Syntax Example	Description
1	Load Pre-Trained Model	`model = hub.KerasLayer(" https://tfhub.de v/...", trainable=False)`	Loads a pre-trained model from TensorFlow Hub.

2	Use Pre-Trained Model as Feature Extractor	`model = tf.keras.Sequent ial([hub.KerasLa yer(...), tf.keras.layers. Dense(...)])`	Extracts features while keeping pre-trained weights frozen.
3	Fine-Tune Pre-Trained Model	`hub.KerasLayer(. .., trainable=True)`	Allows training of pre-trained layers.
4	Preprocess Input for Model	`image = preprocess_funct ion(raw_image)`	Ensures input format matches model expectations.
5	Train Model with Transfer Learning	`model.fit(train_ dataset, epochs=10, validation_data= val_dataset)`	Runs transfer learning with a pre-trained model.

Syntax Explanation:

1. Load Pre-Trained Model

What is Loading a Pre-Trained Model?
Loading a pre-trained model from TensorFlow Hub provides an efficient way to use knowledge learned from large-scale datasets. These models, trained on millions of examples, can be used directly or fine-tuned to solve specific tasks, saving time and computation.

Syntax:
```
import tensorflow_hub as hub
model = hub.KerasLayer("https://tfhub.dev/google/tf2-
preview/mobilenet_v2/classification/4",
trainable=False)
```

Syntax Explanation:
- `hub.KerasLayer(...)`: Loads a pre-trained model as a Keras layer.

- `trainable=False`: Freezes model weights, keeping them unchanged during training.
- Pre-trained models are useful when working with small datasets and limited computing resources.

2. Use Pre-Trained Model as Feature Extractor

What is Feature Extraction?
Feature extraction involves using the lower layers of a pre-trained model to obtain meaningful representations from input data. These extracted features can then be used in a new model for classification or regression tasks.

Syntax:
```
model = tf.keras.Sequential([
    hub.KerasLayer("https://tfhub.dev/google/tf2-preview/mobilenet_v2/classification/4",
trainable=False),
    tf.keras.layers.Dense(10, activation='softmax')
])
```

Syntax Explanation:
- Uses `hub.KerasLayer` to extract high-level image features.
- Adds a `Dense` layer to classify data into 10 categories.
- Freezing the base model prevents overfitting and speeds up training.

3. Fine-Tune Pre-Trained Model

What is Fine-Tuning?
Fine-tuning allows updating a pre-trained model's weights by unfreezing certain layers and training on a new dataset. This method is beneficial when pre-trained features are not fully aligned with the target dataset.

Syntax:
```
hub.KerasLayer("https://tfhub.dev/google/imagenet/mobilenet_v2_100_224/classification/5", trainable=True)
```

Syntax Explanation:

- `trainable=True`: Allows fine-tuning of weights.
- Unlocks layers to update model parameters on a new dataset.
- Best for cases where additional learning improves performance.

4. Preprocess Input for Model

What is Preprocessing Input?
Preprocessing ensures that input images or text are formatted to match the expected format of the pre-trained model. Incorrect preprocessing can lead to suboptimal performance or incorrect predictions.
Syntax:
```
image = preprocess_function(raw_image)
```

Syntax Explanation:

- `preprocess_function(...)`: Converts raw input into model-compatible format.
- Rescales pixel values to [0,1] or normalizes per pre-trained model requirements.
- Essential for ensuring compatibility with pre-trained architectures.

5. Train Model with Transfer Learning

What is Training with Transfer Learning?
Transfer learning applies a pre-trained model to a new task, allowing faster training with limited labeled data. The base model remains frozen initially, with only the new layers being trained.
Syntax:
```
model.fit(train_dataset, epochs=10,
validation_data=val_dataset)
```
Syntax Explanation:

- `train_dataset`: Dataset for model training.
- `epochs=10`: Runs training for 10 iterations.
- `validation_data=val_dataset`: Evaluates model performance on validation data.

Real-Life Project: Fine-Tuning a TensorFlow Hub Model for Custom Classification

Project Goal:

Fine-tune a MobileNetV2 model from TensorFlow Hub to classify custom images.

Steps:

1. **Load Pre-Trained Model:** Use MobileNetV2 as a base model.
2. **Modify Model Architecture:** Add custom dense layers for classification.
3. **Freeze Base Model:** Keep base layers frozen for initial training.
4. **Train Model with New Data:** Train the classifier head while freezing base layers.
5. **Fine-Tune Model:** Unfreeze base layers and train with a lower learning rate.

Code Example:

```python
import tensorflow as tf
import tensorflow_hub as hub
from tensorflow.keras.preprocessing.image import
ImageDataGenerator

# Load pre-trained model
base_model =
hub.KerasLayer("https://tfhub.dev/google/imagenet/mobil
enet_v2_100_224/classification/5", trainable=False)

# Build the model
model = tf.keras.Sequential([
    tf.keras.layers.InputLayer(input_shape=(224, 224,
3)),
    base_model,
    tf.keras.layers.Dense(5, activation='softmax')  #
Custom classification layer
])

# Compile the model
```

```
model.compile(optimizer='adam',
loss='sparse_categorical_crossentropy',
metrics=['accuracy'])

# Train the model
train_datagen = ImageDataGenerator(rescale=1./255)
train_data =
train_datagen.flow_from_directory("./train",
target_size=(224, 224), batch_size=32,
class_mode='sparse')

model.fit(train_data, epochs=5)
```

Expected Output:

```
Improved image classification accuracy using a pre-
trained MobileNetV2 model.
 Improved image classification accuracy using a pre-
trained MobileNetV2 model.
```

Chapter 24: Quantization and Pruning for Efficient Models with TensorFlow

Model efficiency is crucial for deploying deep learning models on edge devices, mobile applications, and low-power environments. Quantization and pruning are two key techniques that help reduce model size and improve inference speed without significantly sacrificing accuracy. This chapter explores how to apply quantization and pruning in TensorFlow to optimize model performance.

Key Characteristics of Quantization and Pruning:

- **Model Compression:** Reduces model size for storage and deployment.
- **Faster Inference:** Optimizes computations for real-time performance.
- **Reduced Power Consumption:** Enables deep learning models to run on low-power devices.
- **Minimal Accuracy Loss:** Maintains acceptable accuracy while reducing model complexity.
- **Works with CPUs, GPUs, and TPUs:** Enhances compatibility across hardware.

Basic Rules for Using Quantization and Pruning:

- Use post-training quantization for reducing model size after training.
- Apply quantization-aware training when training a model to preserve accuracy.
- Prune weights during training to remove redundant connections.
- Convert pruned and quantized models to TensorFlow Lite for edge deployment.
- Evaluate model performance before and after optimization to ensure minimal accuracy loss.

Syntax Table:

SL	Feature	Syntax Example	Description
1	Apply Post-Training Quantization	`converter = tf.lite.TFLiteC onverter.from_k eras_model(mode l)`	Converts model to a quantized format.
2	Quantization-Aware Training	`tf.quantization .experimental_c reate_training_ graph()`	Adds quantization operations during training.
3	Apply Pruning to Model	`tfmot.sparsity. keras.prune_low _magnitude(mode l)`	Prunes the model by reducing weight magnitude.
4	Fine-Tune Pruned Model	`model.fit(train _dataset, epochs=5)`	Trains pruned model to recover accuracy.
5	Convert Model for Deployment	`tf.lite.TFLiteC onverter.from_k eras_model(prun ed_model).conve rt()`	Converts pruned and quantized model to TensorFlow Lite.

Syntax Explanation:

1. Apply Post-Training Quantization

What is Post-Training Quantization?
Post-training quantization reduces model size and accelerates inference by converting model weights and activations into lower precision (e.g., float16 or int8). This technique is particularly useful when deploying models on mobile and edge devices where storage and computation power are limited.

Syntax:
```
import tensorflow as tf
converter =
```

```
tf.lite.TFLiteConverter.from_keras_model(model)
converter.optimizations = [tf.lite.Optimize.DEFAULT]
tflite_model = converter.convert()
```

Syntax Explanation:
- `tf.lite.TFLiteConverter.from_keras_model(model)`:
  Initializes a converter for a trained Keras model.
- `converter.optimizations =`
  `[tf.lite.Optimize.DEFAULT]`: Enables TensorFlow's default
  quantization settings.
- `converter.convert()`: Transforms the model into a quantized
  TensorFlow Lite format.
- Useful for reducing storage space and improving inference
  efficiency.

2. Quantization-Aware Training

What is Quantization-Aware Training?
Quantization-aware training (QAT) incorporates quantization into the
training process, ensuring the model learns to work with lower precision
calculations while retaining accuracy. This helps mitigate potential
accuracy drops that can occur when applying post-training quantization.
Syntax:
```
import tensorflow_model_optimization as tfmot
model =
tfmot.quantization.keras.quantize_model(original_model)
```

Syntax Explanation:
- `tfmot.quantization.keras.quantize_model(model)`:
  Converts an existing model into a quantization-aware version.
- Allows the model to adjust weights for low-precision calculations.
- Best used when post-training quantization results in significant
  accuracy loss.

3. Apply Pruning to Model

What is Model Pruning?
Pruning removes unnecessary weights from a model, making it more efficient without significantly impacting accuracy. By sparsifying the model, pruning reduces storage requirements and speeds up inference.

Syntax:
```
import tensorflow_model_optimization as tfmot
pruned_model =
tfmot.sparsity.keras.prune_low_magnitude(model)
```

Syntax Explanation:
- `prune_low_magnitude(model)`: Applies structured pruning to eliminate redundant weights.
- Increases model sparsity, making computations more efficient.
- Helps improve performance on resource-constrained devices.

4. Fine-Tune Pruned Model

What is Fine-Tuning a Pruned Model?
Fine-tuning a pruned model involves further training after pruning to recover lost accuracy. Since pruning modifies the model structure, additional training helps stabilize weight updates and refine performance.

Syntax:
```
pruned_model.fit(train_dataset, epochs=10,
validation_data=val_dataset)
```

Syntax Explanation:
- `train_dataset`: The dataset used for training.
- `epochs=10`: Runs training for 10 additional iterations.
- `validation_data=val_dataset`: Monitors model performance after pruning.
- Ensures the model maintains accuracy while benefiting from reduced complexity.

5. Convert Model for Deployment

What is Converting a Model for Deployment?
Converting a pruned and quantized model to TensorFlow Lite allows deployment on edge devices, enabling efficient real-time inference.

Syntax:

```
converter =
tf.lite.TFLiteConverter.from_keras_model(pruned_model)
tflite_model = converter.convert()
```

Syntax Explanation:
- Converts optimized models into a compact format suitable for mobile applications.
- Works best when combined with quantization for maximum efficiency.
- Ideal for low-power devices where model size and speed are critical.

Real-Life Project: Deploying an Optimized Model on a Mobile Device
Project Goal:
Optimize a trained image classification model using pruning and quantization, then deploy it to a mobile device.

Steps:
1. **Train a Baseline Model:** Train a neural network on an image classification dataset.
2. **Apply Pruning:** Reduce model size by removing redundant connections while maintaining accuracy.
3. **Perform Post-Training Quantization:** Convert weights and activations to lower precision (int8 or float16).
4. **Convert Model to TensorFlow Lite:** Export the optimized model to .tflite format for mobile deployment.
5. **Deploy to a Mobile Device:** Use TensorFlow Lite Interpreter to run inference on an Android or iOS application.
6. **Evaluate Model Performance:** Measure inference speed and accuracy on mobile hardware.

Code Example:

```python
import tensorflow as tf
import tensorflow_model_optimization as tfmot

# Load pre-trained model
original_model =
tf.keras.applications.MobileNetV2(weights='imagenet',
input_shape=(224, 224, 3))

# Apply pruning
pruned_model =
tfmot.sparsity.keras.prune_low_magnitude(original_model
)

# Apply post-training quantization
converter =
tf.lite.TFLiteConverter.from_keras_model(pruned_model)
converter.optimizations = [tf.lite.Optimize.DEFAULT]
tflite_model = converter.convert()

# Save the optimized model
with open("optimized_model.tflite", "wb") as f:
    f.write(tflite_model)
```

Expected Output:

Reduced model size and improved inference speed while
maintaining high accuracy.

Chapter 25: Image Data Preprocessing in TensorFlow

Image data preprocessing is an essential step in deep learning workflows. Properly formatted and preprocessed image data ensures better model performance, faster training convergence, and improved generalization. TensorFlow provides a range of tools for efficient image preprocessing, including resizing, normalization, augmentation, and dataset pipeline optimization.

Key Characteristics of Image Data Preprocessing:

- **Standardization:** Ensures uniform input data distribution.
- **Augmentation:** Applies transformations to increase dataset diversity.
- **Normalization:** Scales pixel values to a consistent range.
- **Resizing:** Adjusts image dimensions to match model input.
- **Batch Processing:** Optimizes dataset loading and training.

Basic Rules for Image Data Preprocessing:

- Use `tf.image` functions for resizing, flipping, and color adjustments.
- Normalize images to the range [0,1] or [-1,1] for better convergence.
- Apply data augmentation to prevent overfitting.
- Use `tf.data` pipelines for efficient image loading and transformation.
- Ensure image dimensions match the model's expected input shape.

Syntax Table:

SL	Feature	Syntax Example	Description
1	Resize Image	`tf.image.resize(image, (height, width))`	Resizes image to required dimensions.
2	Normalize Pixel Values	`image = image / 255.0`	Scales pixel values to [0,1] range.

3	Data Augmen tation	`tf.image.random_flip` `_left_right(image)`	Randomly flips image horizontally.
4	Convert to Tensor	`image =` `tf.convert_to_tensor` `(image,` `dtype=tf.float32)`	Converts NumPy array or PIL image to TensorFlow tensor.
5	Create Dataset Pipeline	`dataset =` `tf.data.Dataset.from` `_tensor_slices(image` `_paths)`	Loads and processes image dataset efficiently.

Syntax Explanation:

1. Resize Image

What is Image Resizing?
Image resizing is the process of adjusting the dimensions of an image to match the required input shape of a deep learning model. Most models expect a fixed image size, such as 224x224 for MobileNet or 299x299 for InceptionNet.
Syntax:
```
import tensorflow as tf
image = tf.image.resize(image, (224, 224))
```

Syntax Explanation:
- `tf.image.resize(image, (224, 224))`: Rescales the image to 224x224 pixels.
- Keeps aspect ratio if necessary by adding padding (when specified with `preserve_aspect_ratio=True`).
- Essential for maintaining consistency across the dataset.

2. Normalize Pixel Values

What is Normalization?
Normalization scales pixel values to a standard range, improving training stability and convergence speed.

Syntax:
```
image = image / 255.0
```

Syntax Explanation:
- Divides pixel values by `255.0` to scale them to $[0,1]$ range.
- Ensures input values are within a consistent scale for deep learning models.
- Helps in preventing gradient explosion issues.

3. Data Augmentation

What is Data Augmentation?
Data augmentation introduces variations in training images to increase dataset diversity, reducing overfitting.
Syntax:
```
image = tf.image.random_flip_left_right(image)
```

Syntax Explanation:
- `tf.image.random_flip_left_right(image)`: Randomly flips the image horizontally.
- Helps neural networks generalize better by exposing them to different variations.
- Useful for datasets where object orientation is not fixed.

4. Convert to Tensor

What is Converting to Tensor?
Converting an image to a TensorFlow tensor enables efficient computation within the TensorFlow framework.
Syntax:
```
image = tf.convert_to_tensor(image, dtype=tf.float32)
```
Syntax Explanation:
- `tf.convert_to_tensor(image, dtype=tf.float32)`: Converts a NumPy array or PIL image into a TensorFlow tensor.
- Ensures compatibility with TensorFlow operations.
- Optimized for GPU acceleration and parallel processing.

5. Create Dataset Pipeline

What is a Dataset Pipeline?
A dataset pipeline enables efficient image loading and transformation, crucial for handling large-scale datasets.
Syntax:
```
dataset =
tf.data.Dataset.from_tensor_slices(image_paths)
```

Syntax Explanation:
- `tf.data.Dataset.from_tensor_slices(image_paths)`: Creates a dataset from a list of image file paths.
- Enables efficient dataset loading and preprocessing.
- Works well with functions like `map()` for on-the-fly transformations.

Real-Life Project: Image Preprocessing for Classification Model
Project Goal:
Preprocess an image dataset, apply augmentations, and create an efficient pipeline for training an image classification model.
Steps:
1. **Load Image Data:** Read images from disk and convert them to tensors.
2. **Resize and Normalize:** Convert images to a fixed size and scale pixel values.
3. **Apply Data Augmentation:** Introduce random flips, rotations, and brightness adjustments.
4. **Create TensorFlow Dataset:** Optimize dataset loading using `tf.data` pipelines.
5. **Batch and Shuffle:** Efficiently batch and shuffle the dataset to improve training performance.
6. **Train Model:** Use the preprocessed dataset to train a deep learning model.

Code Example:

```python
import tensorflow as tf
import tensorflow_datasets as tfds

def preprocess_image(image, label):
    image = tf.image.resize(image, (224, 224))
    image = image / 255.0  # Normalize pixel values
    image = tf.image.random_flip_left_right(image)
    return image, label

# Load dataset
dataset, info = tfds.load("cats_vs_dogs",
as_supervised=True, with_info=True)
dataset =
dataset["train"].map(preprocess_image).batch(32).shuffl
e(1000)
```

Expected Output:

Efficient image preprocessing pipeline ready for training deep learning models.

Chapter 25: Building Image Classification Models in TensorFlow

Image classification is one of the fundamental applications of deep learning. TensorFlow provides powerful tools to build and train image classification models efficiently. This chapter covers the essential steps for developing an image classification model, from data preprocessing to evaluation and optimization.

Key Characteristics of Image Classification Models:

- **Uses Convolutional Neural Networks (CNNs):** CNNs are the standard architecture for image classification.
- **Data Augmentation Improves Accuracy:** Techniques like rotation and flipping enhance model robustness.
- **Transfer Learning Boosts Performance:** Pretrained models like MobileNet and ResNet speed up training.
- **Batch Normalization and Dropout Prevent Overfitting:** Regularization techniques ensure better generalization.
- **Evaluation Metrics Include Accuracy and Confusion Matrix:** Helps measure model effectiveness.

Basic Rules for Building Image Classification Models:

- Preprocess images to ensure consistency in input size and format.
- Use CNN architectures such as VGG, ResNet, or EfficientNet for better feature extraction.
- Apply data augmentation to improve generalization and reduce overfitting.
- Choose an appropriate loss function (`categorical_crossentropy` for multi-class classification).
- Fine-tune hyperparameters like learning rate, batch size, and number of epochs.

Syntax Table:

SL	Function	Syntax Example	Description
1	Load Dataset	`tf.keras.preprocessing.image_dataset_from_directory()`	Loads images from a directory.
2	Build CNN Model	`tf.keras.Sequential([...])`	Creates a sequential CNN architecture.
3	Compile Model	`model.compile(optimizer='adam', loss='categorical_crossentropy', metrics=['accuracy'])`	Configures the model for training.
4	Train Model	`model.fit(train_data, epochs=10, validation_data=val_data)`	Trains the model with dataset.
5	Evaluate Model	`model.evaluate(test_data)`	Measures model performance on test data.

Syntax Explanation:

1. Load Dataset

What is Loading a Dataset?

Loading an image dataset is the first step in building an image classification model. TensorFlow provides utilities to load and preprocess images efficiently. The dataset must be structured in directories where each subdirectory represents a different class label.

Syntax:

```
train_data =
tf.keras.preprocessing.image_dataset_from_directory(
    "dataset/train", image_size=(224, 224),
batch_size=32)
```

Syntax Explanation:

- `image_dataset_from_directory()`: Loads images from a directory and labels them based on subfolder names.
- `image_size=(224, 224)`: Resizes images to a standard format to ensure uniform input size.
- `batch_size=32`: Defines how many images are processed in each batch to optimize memory usage and training speed.
- This method simplifies dataset handling and allows automatic shuffling and batching.

Example:

```
val_data =
tf.keras.preprocessing.image_dataset_from_directory(
    "dataset/val", image_size=(224, 224),
batch_size=32)
```

Example Explanation:

- Loads validation images from a specified directory.
- Ensures images are preprocessed and resized before passing to the model.
- Helps maintain consistency between training and validation datasets.
- Allows seamless dataset integration with TensorFlow's training pipeline.

2. Build CNN Model

What is a CNN Model?

A Convolutional Neural Network (CNN) is a specialized deep learning model for image classification. CNNs extract hierarchical features from images using convolutional layers, allowing them to recognize patterns such as edges, shapes, and textures.

Syntax:

```
model = tf.keras.Sequential([
    tf.keras.layers.Conv2D(32, (3,3),
activation='relu', input_shape=(224, 224, 3)),
```

```
    tf.keras.layers.MaxPooling2D(2,2),
    tf.keras.layers.Flatten(),
    tf.keras.layers.Dense(128, activation='relu'),
    tf.keras.layers.Dense(10, activation='softmax')
])
```

Syntax Explanation:

- `Conv2D(32, (3,3), activation='relu')`: Adds a convolutional layer with 32 filters that detect image features.
- `MaxPooling2D(2,2)`: Reduces spatial dimensions to retain the most important features.
- `Flatten()`: Converts the feature maps into a 1D vector for classification.
- `Dense(128, activation='relu')`: Adds a fully connected layer to learn non-linear relationships.
- `Dense(10, activation='softmax')`: Output layer for classification into 10 classes.

Example:
```
model = tf.keras.Sequential([...])
```

Example Explanation:

- Defines a simple CNN model using a sequential approach.
- Uses convolutional and pooling layers to extract image features.
- Fully connected layers classify images into their respective categories.
- Can be extended with more layers for improved feature extraction.

3. Compile Model

What is Compiling a Model?

Compiling a model is an essential step in deep learning, where we define the loss function, optimizer, and performance metrics. The model's ability to learn depends on the choices made in this step, as it sets up the mechanism for weight updates during training.

Syntax:
```
model.compile(optimizer='adam',
loss='categorical_crossentropy', metrics=['accuracy'])
```

Syntax Explanation:
- `optimizer='adam'`: Uses the Adam optimizer, which adapts learning rates dynamically for efficient training.
- `loss='categorical_crossentropy'`: Suitable for multi-class classification problems, where each sample belongs to one of several categories.
- `metrics=['accuracy']`: Tracks accuracy as the primary performance measure.
- Ensures the model is ready for training by setting up backpropagation rules.

Example:
```
model.compile(optimizer='sgd',
loss='sparse_categorical_crossentropy',
metrics=['accuracy'])
```

Example Explanation:
- Uses Stochastic Gradient Descent (SGD) as the optimizer.
- Uses `sparse_categorical_crossentropy` for classification tasks with integer-labeled classes.
- Tracks accuracy to evaluate model performance.

4. Train Model

What is Training a Model?
Training a model involves feeding labeled data into the network, computing predictions, comparing them against actual values using a loss function, and adjusting model weights accordingly.

Syntax:
```
model.fit(train_data, epochs=10,
validation_data=val_data)
```

Syntax Explanation:

- `train_data`: The dataset used for training the model.
- `epochs=10`: Specifies the number of full training cycles over the dataset.
- `validation_data=val_data`: Evaluates the model's performance on unseen data.
- Helps refine the model by continuously adjusting weights to minimize loss.

Example:

```
history = model.fit(train_data, epochs=15,
batch_size=32, validation_split=0.2)
```

Example Explanation:

- Trains for 15 epochs using mini-batches of 32 images.
- Uses 20% of the training data as a validation set.
- Stores training history for later visualization of loss and accuracy trends.

5. Evaluate Model

What is Evaluating a Model?

Evaluating a model measures its accuracy and performance on a separate test dataset. This step helps assess whether the model generalizes well to new, unseen images.

Syntax:

```
test_loss, test_acc = model.evaluate(test_data)
```

Syntax Explanation:

- `model.evaluate(test_data)`: Computes loss and accuracy for the test dataset.
- Helps identify overfitting by comparing training and test accuracy.
- Provides final performance metrics before deployment.

Example:

```
loss, accuracy = model.evaluate(val_data,
batch_size=32)
print(f"Validation Accuracy: {accuracy:.4f}")
```

Example Explanation:
- Evaluates the model using mini-batches of 32 images.
- Prints the validation accuracy to compare with training accuracy.
- Helps determine if further optimization or hyperparameter tuning is needed.

Real-Life Project: Image Classification with CNNs

Project Goal:

Build and train a CNN model to classify images into multiple categories.

Steps:
1. **Load and Preprocess Data:** Read images and normalize pixel values.
2. **Build the CNN Model:** Define the architecture using convolutional layers.
3. **Compile the Model:** Choose an optimizer and loss function.
4. **Train the Model:** Fit the model using the training dataset.
5. **Evaluate and Optimize:** Measure performance and fine-tune hyperparameters.

Code Example:

```python
import tensorflow as tf
from tensorflow.keras.preprocessing import
image_dataset_from_directory

# Load datasets
train_data =
image_dataset_from_directory("dataset/train",
image_size=(224, 224), batch_size=32)
val_data = image_dataset_from_directory("dataset/val",
image_size=(224, 224), batch_size=32)

# Build CNN model
model = tf.keras.Sequential([
    tf.keras.layers.Conv2D(32, (3,3),
activation='relu', input_shape=(224, 224, 3)),
    tf.keras.layers.MaxPooling2D(2,2),
    tf.keras.layers.Conv2D(64, (3,3),
```

```python
    activation='relu'),
        tf.keras.layers.MaxPooling2D(2,2),
        tf.keras.layers.Flatten(),
        tf.keras.layers.Dense(128, activation='relu'),
        tf.keras.layers.Dense(10, activation='softmax')
])

# Compile model
model.compile(optimizer='adam',
loss='sparse_categorical_crossentropy',
metrics=['accuracy'])

# Train model
model.fit(train_data, epochs=10,
validation_data=val_data)

# Evaluate model
test_loss, test_acc = model.evaluate(val_data)
print(f"Test Accuracy: {test_acc:.4f}")
```

Expected Output:

```
Training logs followed by final test accuracy.
```

Chapter 26: Object Detection with TensorFlow

Object detection is a crucial task in computer vision that involves identifying and localizing objects within an image. TensorFlow provides powerful tools, including pre-trained models and APIs, to implement object detection efficiently. This chapter explores how to set up, train, and evaluate object detection models using TensorFlow.

Key Characteristics of Object Detection Models:

- **Combination of Classification and Localization:** Identifies objects and determines their positions.
- **Bounding Boxes:** Uses coordinates to define object regions within an image.
- **Popular Architectures:** Faster R-CNN, SSD, and YOLO are commonly used models.
- **Pre-Trained Models:** TensorFlow provides pre-trained models in its Model Zoo.
- **Custom Training Support:** Users can train models on custom datasets for specific applications.

Basic Rules for Implementing Object Detection:

- Use pre-trained models for quick deployment and fine-tuning.
- Ensure images and annotations are in the correct format for training.
- Choose an appropriate architecture based on accuracy and speed trade-offs.
- Apply data augmentation techniques to improve model robustness.
- Regularly evaluate model performance using Intersection over Union (IoU) and mAP (Mean Average Precision).

Syntax Table:

SL	Function	Syntax Example	Description
1	Load Pre-Trained Model	`model = tf.saved_model.load("ssd_mobilenet_v2")`	Loads a pre-trained object detection model.
2	Preprocess Image	`image = tf.image.resize(image, (300, 300))`	Resizes images for compatibility with models.
3	Perform Object Detection	`detections = model(image_tensor)`	Runs the object detection model on an image.
4	Draw Bounding Boxes	`cv2.rectangle(image, box, color, thickness)`	Draws detected object bounding boxes.
5	Train a Custom Model	`model.fit(train_dataset, epochs=10, validation_data=val_dataset)`	Trains an object detection model on a dataset.

Syntax Explanation:

1. Load Pre-Trained Model

What is Loading a Pre-Trained Model?
TensorFlow provides a collection of pre-trained object detection models in its Model Zoo. These models can be used directly for inference or fine-tuned on custom datasets.

Syntax:
```
import tensorflow as tf
model = tf.saved_model.load("ssd_mobilenet_v2")
```

Syntax Explanation:
- `tf.saved_model.load(model_name)`: Loads a pre-trained TensorFlow model.
- Pre-trained models help achieve high accuracy with minimal

training time.

- The `ssd_mobilenet_v2` model is optimized for speed and real-time detection.

Example:
```
model = tf.saved_model.load("faster_rcnn_resnet50")
```

Example Explanation:
- Loads a different object detection model (`Faster R-CNN`), which provides higher accuracy at the cost of speed.
- Suitable for applications requiring precise localization.

2. Preprocess Image

What is Image Preprocessing?
Before feeding an image into an object detection model, it must be resized and normalized to match the model's input requirements.

Syntax:
```
image = tf.image.resize(image, (300, 300))
```

Syntax Explanation:
- `tf.image.resize(image, (300, 300))`: Resizes the image to match the model's expected input size.
- Ensures consistency in detection accuracy across different image dimensions.
- Some models require normalization, converting pixel values to a [0,1] range.

Example:
```
image = tf.image.convert_image_dtype(image, tf.float32)
```

Example Explanation:
- Converts image pixels to float values for better computational performance.
- Improves compatibility with deep learning models that require normalized inputs.

3. Perform Object Detection

What is Performing Object Detection?
Performing object detection involves passing an image through a trained model to identify objects and determine their locations within the image. The model returns bounding box coordinates, class labels, and confidence scores.

Syntax:
```
detections = model(image_tensor)
```

Syntax Explanation:
- `model(image_tensor)`: Runs the input image through the object detection model.
- Outputs detection scores, bounding box coordinates, and class labels.
- Used to identify objects and their positions within the image.
- Can be further refined using confidence thresholds to filter out low-confidence detections.

Example:
```
detections = model(image_tensor)
print(detections['detection_classes'])
```

Example Explanation:
- Runs object detection on the input image.
- Prints the detected class labels.
- Helps analyze the objects identified by the model.

4. Draw Bounding Boxes

What is Drawing Bounding Boxes?
Bounding boxes are rectangular overlays around detected objects. They visually indicate where objects are located in an image.

Syntax:
```
cv2.rectangle(image, box, color, thickness)
```

Syntax Explanation:

- `cv2.rectangle(image, box, color, thickness)`: Draws a rectangle on an image.
- box: The bounding box coordinates (xmin, ymin, xmax, ymax).
- `color`: The color of the rectangle (e.g., (0, 255, 0) for green).
- `thickness`: Defines the width of the bounding box line.
- Helps visualize detected objects effectively.

Example:
```
cv2.rectangle(image, (50, 50), (200, 200), (255, 0, 0), 2)
```

Example Explanation:

- Draws a blue bounding box from (50, 50) to (200, 200).
- Used for marking detected objects on an image.
- Helps in debugging and improving object detection results.

5. Train a Custom Model

What is Training a Custom Object Detection Model?
Training a custom object detection model involves fine-tuning a pre-trained model or training from scratch using labeled datasets. It allows the model to recognize specific objects beyond the default classes.

Syntax:
```
model.fit(train_dataset, epochs=10,
validation_data=val_dataset)
```

Syntax Explanation:

- `train_dataset`: The dataset containing images and corresponding bounding box annotations.
- `epochs=10`: Defines the number of training iterations.
- `validation_data=val_dataset`: Evaluates model performance on unseen data.
- Helps customize models for specific detection tasks.

Example:
```
history = model.fit(train_dataset, epochs=15,
batch_size=8, validation_data=val_dataset)
```

Example Explanation:
- Trains the model for 15 epochs with a batch size of 8.
- Uses validation data to track training performance.
- Helps the model learn object features specific to a custom dataset.

Real-Life Project: Custom Object Detection Using TensorFlow
Project Goal:
Build a custom object detection model to detect specific objects in images or video feeds.
Steps:
1. **Load and Preprocess Data:** Prepare images and annotations for training.
2. **Select a Pre-Trained Model:** Use TensorFlow Model Zoo for a baseline model.
3. **Train on a Custom Dataset:** Fine-tune the model for specific objects.
4. **Evaluate Performance:** Measure accuracy using IoU and mAP.
5. **Deploy and Optimize:** Convert the model for real-time applications.

Code Example:
```
import tensorflow as tf
import cv2
import numpy as np


# Load pre-trained model
model = tf.saved_model.load("ssd_mobilenet_v2")


# Load image
image_path = "sample.jpg"
image = cv2.imread(image_path)
image_resized = tf.image.resize(image, (300, 300))
image_tensor = tf.convert_to_tensor(image_resized,
```

```python
            dtype=tf.uint8)
image_tensor = tf.expand_dims(image_tensor, axis=0)  #
Add batch dimension

# Run object detection
detections = model(image_tensor)

# Draw bounding boxes on detected objects
for i in range(len(detections['detection_scores'])):
    score = detections['detection_scores'][i].numpy()
    if score > 0.5:  # Confidence threshold
        box = detections['detection_boxes'][i].numpy()
        ymin, xmin, ymax, xmax = box
        cv2.rectangle(image, (int(xmin * 300), int(ymin
* 300)),
                      (int(xmax * 300), int(ymax *
300)), (0, 255, 0), 2)

# Display result
cv2.imshow("Object Detection", image)
cv2.waitKey(0)
cv2.destroyAllWindows()
```

Expected Output:

An image with detected objects highlighted using
bounding boxes.

Chapter 27: Building Image Classification Models in TensorFlow

Image classification is a core application of deep learning, enabling models to recognize and categorize images into predefined classes. TensorFlow provides a flexible framework for building image classification models using Convolutional Neural Networks (CNNs) and transfer learning techniques. This chapter explores the essential steps to develop, train, and optimize image classification models in TensorFlow.

Key Characteristics of Image Classification Models:

- **Feature Extraction with CNNs:** Convolutional layers extract hierarchical features from images.
- **Data Augmentation Improves Generalization:** Techniques like flipping and rotation enhance training diversity.
- **Transfer Learning Accelerates Training:** Pre-trained models like MobileNet, ResNet, and EfficientNet improve accuracy.
- **Regularization Reduces Overfitting:** Dropout and batch normalization enhance model robustness.
- **Evaluation Uses Accuracy and Confusion Matrix:** Metrics measure classification performance effectively.

Basic Rules for Building Image Classification Models:

- Preprocess images by resizing and normalizing pixel values.
- Choose a CNN architecture or a pre-trained model for better feature extraction.
- Apply data augmentation to increase training dataset variability.
- Use `categorical_crossentropy` for multi-class classification problems.
- Optimize hyperparameters such as learning rate, batch size, and dropout rate.

Syntax Table:

SL	Function	Syntax Example	Description

1	Load Dataset	`tf.keras.preprocessing`
		`.image_dataset_from_di`
		`rectory()`
			Loads images from a directory.

2	Build CNN Model	`tf.keras.Sequential([.` `..])`	Creates a sequential CNN architecture.

3	Compile Model	`model.compile(optimize`
		`r='adam',`
		`loss='categorical_cros`
		`sentropy',`
		`metrics=['accuracy'])`
			Configures the model for training.

4	Train Model	`model.fit(train_data,`
		`epochs=10,`
		`validation_data=val_da`
		`ta)`
			Trains the model with dataset.

5	Evaluate Model	`model.evaluate(test_da` `ta)`	Measures model performance on test data.

Syntax Explanation:

1. Load Dataset

What is Loading a Dataset?
Loading an image dataset involves reading images from a directory and converting them into a format suitable for training deep learning models.
Syntax:
```
train_data =
tf.keras.preprocessing.image_dataset_from_directory(
    "dataset/train", image_size=(224, 224),
batch_size=32)
```

Syntax Explanation:
- `image_dataset_from_directory()`: Loads images from subdirectories where each folder represents a different class.
- `image_size=(224, 224)`: Resizes images to a fixed size for consistency in model input.
- `batch_size=32`: Defines the number of images processed together during training.

Example:
```
val_data =
tf.keras.preprocessing.image_dataset_from_directory(
    "dataset/val", image_size=(224, 224),
batch_size=32)
```

Example Explanation:
- Loads validation images from the specified directory.
- Ensures images are uniformly resized for evaluation.
- Helps assess model performance on unseen data.

2. Build CNN Model

What is a CNN Model?
A Convolutional Neural Network (CNN) is a deep learning model designed for image classification by learning spatial hierarchies of features.

Syntax:
```
model = tf.keras.Sequential([
    tf.keras.layers.Conv2D(32, (3,3),
activation='relu', input_shape=(224, 224, 3)),
    tf.keras.layers.MaxPooling2D(2,2),
    tf.keras.layers.Flatten(),
    tf.keras.layers.Dense(128, activation='relu'),
    tf.keras.layers.Dense(10, activation='softmax')
])
```

Syntax Explanation:
- `Conv2D(32, (3,3), activation='relu')`: Convolutional layer with 32 filters and ReLU activation.
- `MaxPooling2D(2,2)`: Reduces spatial dimensions while

retaining important features.
- `Flatten()`: Converts feature maps into a single vector.
- `Dense(128, activation='relu')`: Fully connected layer for feature representation.
- `Dense(10, activation='softmax')`: Output layer for classifying images into 10 categories.

Example:
```
model = tf.keras.Sequential([...])
```

Example Explanation:
- Defines a simple CNN model with essential components for image classification.
- Can be expanded with more layers for improved feature extraction.
- Supports different activation functions and dropout layers for optimization.

3. Compile Model

What is Compiling a Model?
Compiling a model is the process of configuring the learning process by defining the optimizer, loss function, and performance metrics. This step ensures the model updates its weights correctly during training to minimize the loss function and maximize accuracy.

Syntax:
```
model.compile(optimizer='adam',
loss='categorical_crossentropy', metrics=['accuracy'])
```

Syntax Explanation:
- `optimizer='adam'`: Uses the Adam optimizer, which adapts the learning rate dynamically for efficient convergence.
- `loss='categorical_crossentropy'`: Suitable for multi-class classification problems.
- `metrics=['accuracy']`: Tracks accuracy as the primary evaluation metric.

- Ensures the model is ready for training by setting up backpropagation and gradient updates.

Example:
```
model.compile(optimizer='sgd',
loss='sparse_categorical_crossentropy',
metrics=['accuracy'])
```

Example Explanation:
- Uses Stochastic Gradient Descent (SGD) as the optimizer.
- Uses `sparse_categorical_crossentropy` for classification tasks with integer-labeled classes.
- Tracks accuracy to monitor performance during training.

4. Train Model

What is Training a Model?
Training a model involves feeding it labeled data, allowing it to adjust weights through backpropagation, and minimizing the loss function iteratively over multiple epochs.

Syntax:
```
model.fit(train_data, epochs=10,
validation_data=val_data)
```

Syntax Explanation:
- `train_data`: The dataset used for training the model.
- `epochs=10`: Defines the number of full training cycles over the dataset.
- `validation_data=val_data`: Evaluates the model's performance on unseen data.
- Adjusts model weights to minimize loss and improve predictions.

Example:
```
history = model.fit(train_data, epochs=15,
batch_size=32, validation_split=0.2)
```

Example Explanation:
- Trains for 15 epochs with mini-batches of 32 images.
- Uses 20% of the training data as a validation set.
- Stores training history for later visualization of loss and accuracy trends.

5. Evaluate Model

What is Evaluating a Model?
Evaluating a model measures its accuracy and performance on a separate test dataset. This step helps assess whether the model generalizes well to new, unseen images.

Syntax:
```
test_loss, test_acc = model.evaluate(test_data)
```

Syntax Explanation:
- `model.evaluate(test_data)`: Computes loss and accuracy for the test dataset.
- Helps identify overfitting by comparing training and test accuracy.
- Provides final performance metrics before deployment.

Example:
```
loss, accuracy = model.evaluate(val_data,
batch_size=32)
print(f"Validation Accuracy: {accuracy:.4f}")
```

Example Explanation:
- Evaluates the model using mini-batches of 32 images.
- Prints the validation accuracy to compare with training accuracy.
- Helps determine if further optimization or hyperparameter tuning is needed.

Real-Life Project: Image Classification Using TensorFlow
Project Goal:
Train a CNN model to classify images into predefined categories and evaluate its performance.

Steps:

1. **Load and Preprocess Data:** Read images and apply normalization.
2. **Build the CNN Model:** Construct a convolutional architecture.
3. **Compile the Model:** Define the optimizer and loss function.
4. **Train the Model:** Train the network using labeled images.
5. **Evaluate and Optimize:** Assess performance and fine-tune parameters.

Code Example:

```python
import tensorflow as tf
from tensorflow.keras.preprocessing import
image_dataset_from_directory

# Load dataset
train_data =
image_dataset_from_directory("dataset/train",
image_size=(224, 224), batch_size=32)
val_data = image_dataset_from_directory("dataset/val",
image_size=(224, 224), batch_size=32)

# Build CNN model
model = tf.keras.Sequential([
    tf.keras.layers.Conv2D(32, (3,3),
activation='relu', input_shape=(224, 224, 3)),
    tf.keras.layers.MaxPooling2D(2,2),
    tf.keras.layers.Conv2D(64, (3,3),
activation='relu'),
    tf.keras.layers.MaxPooling2D(2,2),
    tf.keras.layers.Flatten(),
    tf.keras.layers.Dense(128, activation='relu'),
    tf.keras.layers.Dense(10, activation='softmax')
])

# Compile model
model.compile(optimizer='adam',
loss='sparse_categorical_crossentropy',
```

```python
        metrics=['accuracy'])

# Train model
model.fit(train_data, epochs=10,
validation_data=val_data)

# Evaluate model
test_loss, test_acc = model.evaluate(val_data)
print(f"Test Accuracy: {test_acc:.4f}")
```

Expected Output:

Training logs followed by final test accuracy.

Chapter 28: Semantic and Instance Segmentation in TensorFlow

Semantic and instance segmentation are key tasks in computer vision, allowing models to differentiate between objects and their boundaries. Semantic segmentation classifies each pixel in an image, while instance segmentation assigns different labels to separate objects of the same class. TensorFlow provides powerful tools, including the TensorFlow Model Garden and Keras, to build and train segmentation models effectively.

Key Characteristics of Segmentation Models:

- **Pixel-wise Classification:** Assigns each pixel a label corresponding to an object class.
- **Semantic Segmentation:** Groups pixels belonging to the same class without distinguishing between objects.
- **Instance Segmentation:** Differentiates multiple objects of the same class.
- **Common Architectures:** U-Net, DeepLabV3+, Mask R-CNN are widely used models.
- **Pre-Trained Models Available:** TensorFlow provides pre-trained segmentation models for faster deployment.

Basic Rules for Implementing Segmentation Models:

- Use a pre-trained model for better performance on small datasets.
- Ensure images and masks are correctly formatted before training.
- Choose a suitable loss function like `categorical_crossentropy` or `dice loss`.
- Apply data augmentation techniques to improve generalization.
- Evaluate models using IoU (Intersection over Union) or Dice coefficient.

Syntax Table:

SL	Function	Syntax Example	Description
1	Load Pre-Trained Model	`model = tf.keras.applications.DeepLabV3(weights='imagenet')`	Loads a pre-trained semantic segmentation model.
2	Preprocess Image	`image = tf.image.resize(image, (256, 256))`	Resizes image for model input.
3	Train Segmentation Model	`model.fit(train_dataset, epochs=10, validation_data=val_dataset)`	Trains a segmentation model on custom data.
4	Predict Segmentation Mask	`mask = model.predict(image_batch)`	Generates a segmentation mask from input images.
5	Evaluate Model Performance	`iou = compute_iou(y_true, y_pred)`	Calculates Intersection over Union (IoU) metric.

Syntax Explanation:

1. Load Pre-Trained Model

What is a Pre-Trained Model?
Pre-trained models are deep learning models that have been trained on large datasets, making them useful for transfer learning. TensorFlow provides pre-trained segmentation models like DeepLabV3 and Mask R-CNN.

Syntax:
```
import tensorflow as tf
model = tf.keras.applications.DeepLabV3(weights='imagenet')
```

Syntax Explanation:
- `tf.keras.applications.DeepLabV3(weights='imagenet')`: Loads a pre-trained DeepLabV3 model trained on ImageNet.

- Useful for segmenting images into multiple object categories.
- Reduces training time when working with limited datasets.

Example:
```
model =
tf.keras.applications.DeepLabV3(include_top=False,
weights='imagenet')
```

Example Explanation:
- Removes the top classification layers to use the model for feature extraction.
- Allows for fine-tuning on a custom dataset.

2. Preprocess Image

What is Image Preprocessing?
Preprocessing ensures that input images match the required dimensions and format expected by the segmentation model.

Syntax:
```
image = tf.image.resize(image, (256, 256))
```

Syntax Explanation:
- `tf.image.resize(image, (256, 256))`: Resizes the input image to 256x256 pixels.
- Helps standardize input dimensions across the dataset.
- Required for efficient training and inference.

Example:
```
image = tf.image.convert_image_dtype(image, tf.float32)
```

Example Explanation:
- Converts image pixels to floating-point format for improved computation.
- Normalizes pixel values, which helps improve model convergence.

3. Train Segmentation Model

What is Training a Segmentation Model?
Training a segmentation model involves feeding it with labeled image-mask pairs, adjusting weights using backpropagation, and optimizing the model's ability to distinguish objects from the background.

Syntax:
```
model.fit(train_dataset, epochs=10,
validation_data=val_dataset)
```

Syntax Explanation:
- train_dataset: A dataset containing images and corresponding segmentation masks.
- epochs=10: Defines the number of complete passes over the training dataset.
- validation_data=val_dataset: Evaluates performance using unseen validation data.
- Adjusts model weights iteratively to minimize segmentation loss.

Example:
```
history = model.fit(train_dataset, epochs=15,
batch_size=16, validation_split=0.2)
```

Example Explanation:
- Trains for 15 epochs with mini-batches of 16 images.
- Uses 20% of the training data for validation.
- Stores training history for visualizing loss and IoU trends.

4. Predict Segmentation Mask

What is Predicting a Segmentation Mask?
Once trained, a segmentation model can generate masks that highlight detected objects within an image.

Syntax:
```
mask = model.predict(image_batch)
```

Syntax Explanation:
- `model.predict(image_batch)`: Generates a segmentation mask for the given image(s).
- The output is a tensor representing pixel-wise classifications.
- Used for real-time object segmentation in various applications.

Example:
```
predicted_mask = model.predict(test_image)
predicted_mask = tf.argmax(predicted_mask, axis=-1)
```

Example Explanation:
- Runs inference on a test image to generate a predicted mask.
- Uses argmax to extract the most likely class for each pixel.
- Produces a binary or multi-class segmentation map.

5. Evaluate Model Performance

What is Evaluating a Segmentation Model?
Evaluating a segmentation model measures how well its predictions align with ground-truth masks using metrics like IoU (Intersection over Union) and Dice coefficient.

Syntax:
```
iou = compute_iou(y_true, y_pred)
```

Syntax Explanation:
- `compute_iou(y_true, y_pred)`: Calculates the IoU score, a measure of overlap between predicted and actual masks.
- Helps determine how accurately the model identifies object boundaries.
- Used for benchmarking segmentation models.

Example:
```
def compute_iou(y_true, y_pred):
    intersection = tf.reduce_sum(y_true * y_pred)
    union = tf.reduce_sum(y_true + y_pred) -
intersection
    return intersection / union
```

Example Explanation:

- Computes IoU by dividing the intersection of predicted and true masks by their union.
- Provides a numeric evaluation of segmentation accuracy.
- Helps track model improvements during training.

Real-Life Project: Semantic Segmentation for Medical Imaging

Project Goal:

Develop a deep learning model to segment medical images, such as CT scans or X-rays, to detect abnormalities.

Steps:

1. **Load and Preprocess Data:** Prepare medical imaging datasets with pixel-wise labels.
2. **Select a Model:** Use a pre-trained U-Net or DeepLabV3 model for segmentation.
3. **Train on Custom Data:** Fine-tune the model using domain-specific datasets.
4. **Evaluate Performance:** Measure accuracy using IoU and Dice coefficient.
5. **Deploy the Model:** Use the trained model for real-time segmentation tasks.

Code Example:

```
import tensorflow as tf
import numpy as np

# Load dataset
(x_train, y_train), (x_val, y_val) =
load_medical_segmentation_dataset()

# Preprocess dataset
x_train = tf.image.resize(x_train, (256, 256)) / 255.0
x_val = tf.image.resize(x_val, (256, 256)) / 255.0

# Define U-Net model
model = tf.keras.models.Sequential([
```

```python
    tf.keras.layers.Conv2D(64, (3,3),
activation='relu', padding='same', input_shape=(256,
256, 3)),
    tf.keras.layers.MaxPooling2D(2,2),
    tf.keras.layers.Conv2DTranspose(64, (3,3),
activation='relu', padding='same'),
    tf.keras.layers.Conv2D(1, (1,1),
activation='sigmoid')
])

# Compile model
model.compile(optimizer='adam',
loss='binary_crossentropy', metrics=['accuracy'])

# Train model
model.fit(x_train, y_train, epochs=10,
validation_data=(x_val, y_val))

# Evaluate model
loss, accuracy = model.evaluate(x_val, y_val)
print(f"Validation Accuracy: {accuracy:.4f}")
```

Expected Output:

Training logs showing loss and accuracy followed by
final validation accuracy.

Chapter 29: Generative Adversarial Networks (GANs) in TensorFlow

Generative Adversarial Networks (GANs) are a class of deep learning models used for generating realistic data, such as images, videos, and text. GANs consist of two competing neural networks: a generator and a discriminator. The generator creates synthetic data, while the discriminator evaluates its authenticity. TensorFlow provides powerful tools to build and train GANs effectively.

Key Characteristics of GANs:

- **Consist of Two Networks:** The generator creates fake data, and the discriminator distinguishes between real and fake data.
- **Adversarial Training:** Both networks improve by competing against each other.
- **Used for Data Generation:** Common applications include image synthesis, super-resolution, and style transfer.
- **Common Architectures:** DCGAN, CycleGAN, and StyleGAN are widely used.
- **Challenges:** Training can be unstable due to mode collapse and vanishing gradients.

Basic Rules for Implementing GANs:

- Use separate neural networks for the generator and discriminator.
- Optimize using adversarial loss functions like binary cross-entropy.
- Ensure balanced training between generator and discriminator to prevent one from dominating.
- Use techniques like batch normalization and dropout to stabilize training.
- Evaluate GAN performance using qualitative metrics and Fréchet Inception Distance (FID).

Syntax Table:

SL	Function	Syntax Example	Description
1	Define Generator Model	`generator = tf.keras.Sequentia l([...])`	Creates a neural network to generate fake data.
2	Define Discriminator Model	`discriminator = tf.keras.Sequentia l([...])`	Builds a neural network to classify real vs. fake.
3	Compile Discriminator	`discriminator.comp ile(optimizer='ada m', loss='binary_cross entropy')`	Configures the discriminator model for training.
4	Train GAN	`gan.fit(dataset, epochs=50)`	Trains both generator and discriminator.
5	Generate Fake Samples	`generated_images = generator.predict( noise_vector)`	Uses the trained generator to create new samples.

Syntax Explanation:

1. Define Generator Model

What is a Generator Model?
The generator is a neural network that takes random noise as input and generates synthetic data that mimics real data.

Syntax:
```
import tensorflow as tf
generator = tf.keras.Sequential([
    tf.keras.layers.Dense(128, activation='relu',
input_shape=(100,)),
    tf.keras.layers.BatchNormalization(),
    tf.keras.layers.Dense(784, activation='sigmoid'),
    tf.keras.layers.Reshape((28, 28, 1))
])
```

Syntax Explanation:

- `Dense(128, activation='relu')`: Fully connected layer with ReLU activation for feature extraction.
- `BatchNormalization()`: Stabilizes training by normalizing activations.
- `Dense(784, activation='sigmoid')`: Outputs a flattened image representation.
- `Reshape((28, 28, 1))`: Reshapes output to match the dimensions of an image.

Example:

```
noise = tf.random.normal([1, 100])
generated_image = generator(noise)
```

Example Explanation:

- Generates an image from a random noise vector of size 100.
- Produces an output resembling real images.

2. Define Discriminator Model

What is a Discriminator Model?

The discriminator is a neural network that classifies whether an input image is real or fake.

Syntax:

```
discriminator = tf.keras.Sequential([
    tf.keras.layers.Flatten(input_shape=(28, 28, 1)),
    tf.keras.layers.Dense(128, activation='relu'),
    tf.keras.layers.Dense(1, activation='sigmoid')
])
```

Syntax Explanation:

- `Flatten(input_shape=(28, 28, 1))`: Converts image input into a vector.
- `Dense(128, activation='relu')`: Extracts features for classification.
- `Dense(1, activation='sigmoid')`: Outputs probability of being real or fake.

Example:
```
discriminator.compile(optimizer='adam',
loss='binary_crossentropy')
```

Example Explanation:
- Uses binary cross-entropy loss for binary classification.
- Helps train the model to distinguish between real and fake images.

3. Compile Discriminator

What is Compiling the Discriminator?
Compiling the discriminator involves configuring its optimizer and loss function to ensure it effectively distinguishes between real and fake data. The discriminator learns to classify inputs accurately by updating its weights during training.

Syntax:
```
discriminator.compile(optimizer='adam',
loss='binary_crossentropy', metrics=['accuracy'])
```

Syntax Explanation:
- `optimizer='adam'`: Uses the Adam optimizer, which adjusts learning rates dynamically for efficient training.
- `loss='binary_crossentropy'`: Measures how well the discriminator differentiates real and fake samples.
- `metrics=['accuracy']`: Tracks how often the discriminator correctly classifies inputs.
- Helps stabilize training by preventing one model from overpowering the other.

Example:
```
discriminator.compile(optimizer=tf.keras.optimizers.RMS
prop(learning_rate=0.0002), loss='binary_crossentropy')
```

Example Explanation:
- Uses the RMSprop optimizer with a small learning rate to prevent instability.
- Trains the discriminator to improve classification accuracy over time.

4. Train GAN

What is Training a GAN?
Training a GAN involves an alternating optimization process where the generator creates synthetic data, and the discriminator learns to distinguish it from real data. The generator aims to fool the discriminator, while the discriminator refines its ability to detect fake samples.

Syntax:
```
gan.fit(train_dataset, epochs=50)
```

Syntax Explanation:
- `train_dataset`: The dataset containing real training images.
- `epochs=50`: Defines the number of times the GAN iterates over the dataset.
- The generator and discriminator are updated alternately to improve their performance.
- Helps produce more realistic synthetic images over time.

Example:
```
for epoch in range(50):
    noise = tf.random.normal([64, 100])
    generated_images = generator(noise)

    real_labels = tf.ones((64, 1))
    fake_labels = tf.zeros((64, 1))

    discriminator.train_on_batch(real_images,
real_labels)
    discriminator.train_on_batch(generated_images,
fake_labels)
    gan.train_on_batch(noise, real_labels)
```

Example Explanation:
- Generates a batch of fake images using the generator.
- Trains the discriminator on both real and fake samples.
- Updates the generator by encouraging it to produce more convincing images.

5. Generate Fake Samples

What is Generating Fake Samples?
Once the GAN is trained, the generator can create synthetic images that resemble real ones by transforming random noise into meaningful patterns.

Syntax:
```
generated_images = generator.predict(noise_vector)
```

Syntax Explanation:
- `generator.predict(noise_vector)`: Feeds random noise into the trained generator to produce images.
- Generates new samples that resemble the training dataset.
- Helps in applications such as image synthesis, style transfer, and data augmentation.

Example:
```
noise = tf.random.normal([5, 100])
generated_images = generator(noise)
```

Example Explanation:
- Generates five synthetic images from random noise.
- Can be visualized using Matplotlib or OpenCV to assess quality.
- Demonstrates the generator's ability to create realistic data.

Real-Life Project: Training a GAN for Handwritten Digit Generation
Project Goal:
Build and train a GAN model to generate synthetic images of handwritten digits using TensorFlow.

Steps:
1. **Load and Preprocess Data:** Use the MNIST dataset for training.
2. **Build the Generator and Discriminator Models:** Define architectures for both networks.
3. **Train the GAN:** Train the model using adversarial loss.
4. **Generate New Images:** Use the trained generator to create realistic samples.
5. **Evaluate Performance:** Assess the quality of generated images.

Code Example:

```python
import tensorflow as tf
import numpy as np

def build_generator():
    model = tf.keras.Sequential([
        tf.keras.layers.Dense(128, activation='relu',
input_shape=(100,)),
        tf.keras.layers.BatchNormalization(),
        tf.keras.layers.Dense(784,
activation='sigmoid'),
        tf.keras.layers.Reshape((28, 28, 1))
    ])
    return model

def build_discriminator():
    model = tf.keras.Sequential([
        tf.keras.layers.Flatten(input_shape=(28, 28,
1)),
        tf.keras.layers.Dense(128, activation='relu'),
        tf.keras.layers.Dense(1, activation='sigmoid')
    ])
    model.compile(optimizer='adam',
loss='binary_crossentropy')
    return model

generator = build_generator()
discriminator = build_discriminator()

# Define GAN
class GAN(tf.keras.Model):
    def __init__(self, generator, discriminator):
        super(GAN, self).__init__()
        self.generator = generator
        self.discriminator = discriminator
```

```python
    def call(self, inputs):
        generated_images = self.generator(inputs)
        return self.discriminator(generated_images)

# Instantiate and compile GAN
gan = GAN(generator, discriminator)
gan.compile(optimizer='adam',
loss='binary_crossentropy')

# Train GAN
(train_images, _), (_, _) =
tf.keras.datasets.mnist.load_data()
train_images = (train_images.astype(np.float32) -
127.5) / 127.5   # Normalize
train_images = np.expand_dims(train_images, axis=-1)

gan.fit(train_images, epochs=10, batch_size=64)

# Generate new images
noise = tf.random.normal([5, 100])
generated_images = generator(noise)
```

Expected Output:

Training logs followed by newly generated images
resembling handwritten digits.

Chapter 30: Text Data Preprocessing in TensorFlow

Text preprocessing is a crucial step in Natural Language Processing (NLP) to prepare raw text for deep learning models. TensorFlow provides various utilities for tokenization, text vectorization, and cleaning text data before feeding it into models. This chapter covers key techniques for text preprocessing in TensorFlow.

Key Characteristics of Text Preprocessing:

- **Tokenization:** Converts text into a sequence of tokens (words or subwords).
- **Text Vectorization:** Transforms words into numerical representations for models.
- **Padding and Truncation:** Ensures input sequences have a uniform length.
- **Lowercasing and Removing Punctuation:** Standardizes text format.
- **Handling Out-of-Vocabulary (OOV) Words:** Manages unseen words during inference.

Basic Rules for Text Preprocessing:

- Use `TextVectorization` for efficient text tokenization and embedding preparation.
- Convert words into numerical representations like word embeddings or one-hot encoding.
- Ensure all text sequences have the same length by applying padding or truncation.
- Remove unnecessary characters, punctuation, and stopwords when required.
- Handle OOV words to prevent errors during inference.

Syntax Table:

SL	Function	Syntax Example	Description
1	Tokenize Text	`tokenizer = tf.keras.preprocessing.text.Tokenizer()`	Creates a tokenizer for text tokenization.

2	Convert Text to Sequences	`sequences = tokenizer.texts_to_se quences(sentences)`	Converts words into integer sequences.
3	Pad Sequences	`padded_sequences = pad_sequences(sequenc es, maxlen=10)`	Ensures uniform sequence length.
4	Use TextVectoriz ation Layer	`vectorizer = TextVectorization(out put_mode='int')`	Automatically tokenizes and vectorizes text.
5	Handle OOV Words	`tokenizer = Tokenizer(oov_token=' <OOV>')`	Manages words not seen during training.

Syntax Explanation:

1. Tokenize Text

What is Tokenization?

Tokenization splits raw text into individual words or subwords and assigns each token a unique integer identifier. It is essential for NLP tasks because deep learning models cannot process raw text directly. Instead, they require numerical representations of words or subwords.

Syntax:

```
import tensorflow as tf
from tensorflow.keras.preprocessing.text import
Tokenizer

tokenizer = Tokenizer(num_words=10000)
```

Syntax Explanation:

- `Tokenizer(num_words=10000)`: Keeps only the most frequent 10,000 words in the dataset to limit vocabulary size and reduce computational complexity.
- Converts text into integer representations suitable for deep learning models.
- Helps reduce sparsity and makes text data manageable.

Example:
```
sentences = ["Hello world!", "TensorFlow makes NLP
easy"]
tokenizer.fit_on_texts(sentences)
print(tokenizer.word_index)
```

Example Explanation:
- Processes sentences and builds a vocabulary dictionary where each word is assigned a unique index.
- Assigns lower indices to more frequent words, optimizing memory usage.
- Allows models to efficiently process text input for training.

2. Convert Text to Sequences
What is Text to Sequence Conversion?
Text-to-sequence conversion replaces words in a sentence with their respective integer indices, forming a sequence that deep learning models can process. This is a crucial step in NLP workflows as it enables word embeddings and sequence modeling.

Syntax:
```
sequences = tokenizer.texts_to_sequences(sentences)
```
Syntax Explanation:
- `texts_to_sequences(sentences)`: Converts a list of sentences into a list of sequences where each word is replaced by its corresponding index from the tokenizer's vocabulary.
- Helps convert text into a numerical format required for deep learning.
- Ensures consistent representation of words for training models.

Example:
```
print(sequences)
```
Example Explanation:
- Outputs a list of integer sequences representing tokenized sentences.
- Ensures uniform representation of words across different sentences.
- Makes text input suitable for embedding layers in deep learning models.

3. Pad Sequences

What is Padding Sequences?
Deep learning models expect fixed-length inputs, but text sequences often have varying lengths. Padding ensures that all sequences have the same length by adding zeros or truncating longer sequences.

Syntax:
```
from tensorflow.keras.preprocessing.sequence import pad_sequences
padded_sequences = pad_sequences(sequences, maxlen=10, padding='post')
```

Syntax Explanation:
- `pad_sequences(sequences, maxlen=10)`: Ensures all sequences are of length 10 by adding padding where necessary.
- `padding='post'`: Adds padding at the end of the sequence instead of the beginning.
- Prevents issues arising from varying input lengths in deep learning models.

Example:
```
print(padded_sequences)
```

Example Explanation:
- Displays the padded sequences where shorter sentences are filled with zeros at the end.
- Standardizes text length for model training and inference.
- Prevents unexpected errors caused by variable-length input.

4. Use TextVectorization Layer

What is TextVectorization?
The TextVectorization layer in TensorFlow automatically tokenizes and converts text into integer sequences, simplifying preprocessing pipelines.

Syntax:
```
from tensorflow.keras.layers import TextVectorization
vectorizer = TextVectorization(output_mode='int',
max_tokens=10000)
```

Syntax Explanation:
- `output_mode='int'`: Converts text into integer sequences.
- `max_tokens=10000`: Limits the vocabulary size to optimize model performance.
- Simplifies preprocessing by handling tokenization and vectorization in one step.

Example:
```
vectorizer.adapt(sentences)
vectorized_text = vectorizer(sentences)
print(vectorized_text)
```

Example Explanation:
- Automatically tokenizes and converts text to integer sequences.
- Makes text processing more efficient and integrated within TensorFlow pipelines.
- Useful for deep learning models requiring end-to-end preprocessing.

5. Handle OOV Words

What is Handling Out-of-Vocabulary (OOV) Words?

OOV words are words that are not present in the training vocabulary. Handling OOV words prevents errors when processing new text data.

Syntax:
```
tokenizer = Tokenizer(oov_token='<OOV>')
```

Syntax Explanation:
- `oov_token='<OOV>'`: Assigns a placeholder token to unknown words.
- Prevents model crashes when encountering new words during inference.
- Ensures a fallback mechanism for handling words outside the vocabulary.

Example:

```
new_sentences = ["I love AI"]
sequences = tokenizer.texts_to_sequences(new_sentences)
print(sequences)
```

Example Explanation:

- Converts unknown words into a predefined OOV token.
- Allows models to handle unseen words without failing.
- Essential for NLP tasks involving dynamic and evolving vocabularies.

Real-Life Project: Sentiment Analysis Preprocessing

Project Goal:

Prepare a dataset for sentiment analysis by applying text preprocessing techniques in TensorFlow.

Steps:

1. **Load and Preprocess Data:** Clean and tokenize text samples.
2. **Convert Text to Sequences:** Replace words with integer indices.
3. **Apply Padding:** Ensure uniform sequence length.
4. **Use Word Embeddings:** Transform words into dense vectors.
5. **Feed Preprocessed Data into an NLP Model:** Train a classifier on the processed text.

Code Example:

```
import tensorflow as tf
from tensorflow.keras.preprocessing.text import
Tokenizer
from tensorflow.keras.preprocessing.sequence import
pad_sequences

# Sample dataset
sentences = [
    "I love TensorFlow!",
    "Deep learning is amazing.",
    "NLP models are powerful.",
    "Text preprocessing is important."
]
```

```
# Tokenization
tokenizer = Tokenizer(oov_token="<OOV>")
tokenizer.fit_on_texts(sentences)
sequences = tokenizer.texts_to_sequences(sentences)

# Padding
padded_sequences = pad_sequences(sequences, maxlen=5,
padding='post')

print("Word Index:", tokenizer.word_index)
print("Padded Sequences:", padded_sequences)
```

Expected Output:

```
Word Index: {'<OOV>': 1, 'text': 2, 'learning': 3,
'tensorflow': 4, 'models': 5, 'deep': 6, 'nlp': 7, ...}
Padded Sequences: [[2, 4, 0, 0, 0], [6, 3, 0, 0, 0],
[7, 5, 0, 0, 0], [2, 8, 0, 0, 0]]
```

Chapter 31: Implementing RNNs and LSTMs in TensorFlow

Recurrent Neural Networks (RNNs) and Long Short-Term Memory (LSTM) networks are specialized deep learning architectures for sequential data, such as time series, speech, and natural language processing (NLP). TensorFlow provides built-in layers and utilities for implementing RNNs and LSTMs efficiently. This chapter explores the key concepts, implementation, and optimization techniques for training these models in TensorFlow.

Key Characteristics of RNNs and LSTMs:

- **Designed for Sequential Data:** RNNs process data with a temporal or ordered structure.
- **Memory Retention:** LSTMs solve the vanishing gradient problem by maintaining long-term dependencies.
- **Common Use Cases:** Language modeling, speech recognition, stock price prediction.
- **Built-in Layers in TensorFlow:** SimpleRNN, LSTM, and GRU layers for flexible architecture design.
- **Optimized for Backpropagation Through Time (BPTT):** Handles gradient flow efficiently.

Basic Rules for Implementing RNNs and LSTMs:

- Use Embedding layers for NLP tasks to convert words into vector representations.
- Use LSTMs or GRUs instead of vanilla RNNs for better long-term memory retention.
- Normalize and preprocess input sequences to improve model convergence.
- Use dropout and recurrent dropout to prevent overfitting.
- Tune hyperparameters like learning rate, sequence length, and number of recurrent layers.

Syntax Table:

SL	Function	Syntax Example	Description
1	Define RNN Layer	`tf.keras.layers.Si` `mpleRNN(64,` `return_sequences=T` `rue)`	Creates a simple RNN layer.
2	Define LSTM Layer	`tf.keras.layers.LS` `TM(128,` `return_sequences=F` `alse)`	Creates an LSTM layer with 128 hidden units.
3	Compile RNN Model	`model.compile(opti` `mizer='adam',` `loss='mse')`	Configures the model for training.
4	Train RNN Model	`model.fit(train_da` `ta, epochs=10,` `validation_data=va` `l_data)`	Trains the RNN model with dataset.
5	Make Predictions	`predictions =` `model.predict(test` `_data)`	Generates predictions using the trained model.

Syntax Explanation:

1. Define RNN Layer

What is an RNN Layer?
A Recurrent Neural Network (RNN) layer processes sequential data by maintaining hidden states across time steps. The SimpleRNN layer in TensorFlow allows the creation of basic RNNs.

Syntax:
```
import tensorflow as tf

rnn_layer = tf.keras.layers.SimpleRNN(64,
return_sequences=True, activation='tanh')
```

Syntax Explanation:

- `SimpleRNN(64)`: Defines an RNN layer with 64 hidden units.
- `return_sequences=True`: Outputs the full sequence of hidden states.
- `activation='tanh'`: Uses the tanh activation function to process sequential data.
- Helps capture short-term dependencies in time-series or NLP tasks.

Example:
```
rnn_model = tf.keras.Sequential([
    tf.keras.layers.SimpleRNN(64, input_shape=(100,
1)),
    tf.keras.layers.Dense(1)
])
```

Example Explanation:
- Creates an RNN model with a single recurrent layer.
- Takes input of shape (100,1), representing a sequence of 100 time steps.
- Outputs a single value, suitable for regression tasks.

2. Define LSTM Layer

What is an LSTM Layer?
LSTMs improve on standard RNNs by introducing gating mechanisms that regulate information flow, preventing vanishing gradients.

Syntax:
```
lstm_layer = tf.keras.layers.LSTM(128,
return_sequences=False)
```

Syntax Explanation:
- `LSTM(128)`: Creates an LSTM layer with 128 hidden units.
- `return_sequences=False`: Outputs only the last hidden state.
- Manages long-term dependencies better than vanilla RNNs.

Example:
```
lstm_model = tf.keras.Sequential([
    tf.keras.layers.LSTM(128, input_shape=(100, 1)),
    tf.keras.layers.Dense(1)
])
```

Example Explanation:
- Uses an LSTM layer for sequential input processing.
- Suitable for tasks requiring long-term memory retention, like NLP.

3. Compile RNN Model

What is Compiling an RNN Model?
Compiling an RNN model is the process of defining how the model will learn by specifying the optimizer, loss function, and evaluation metrics. This step prepares the model for training by configuring the weight update mechanism.

Syntax:
```
model.compile(optimizer='adam', loss='mse',
metrics=['mae'])
```

Syntax Explanation:
- `optimizer='adam'`: Uses the Adam optimizer, which adapts learning rates dynamically.
- `loss='mse'`: Applies Mean Squared Error as the loss function, suitable for regression tasks.
- `metrics=['mae']`: Tracks Mean Absolute Error as an additional evaluation metric.
- Helps in stabilizing training and improving the learning process.

Example:
```
model.compile(optimizer=tf.keras.optimizers.RMSprop(lea
rning_rate=0.001), loss='mse')
```

Example Explanation:
- Uses the RMSprop optimizer with a custom learning rate.
- Optimized for handling sequential data with non-stationary patterns.

4. Train RNN Model

What is Training an RNN Model?
Training an RNN model involves feeding it input sequences, adjusting its weights through backpropagation, and optimizing the loss function to improve predictions.

Syntax:
```
model.fit(train_data, epochs=10, batch_size=32,
validation_data=val_data)
```
Syntax Explanation:
- `train_data`: The dataset used for training.
- `epochs=10`: Runs training for 10 complete passes over the dataset.
- `batch_size=32`: Processes data in mini-batches of 32 samples for stability.
- `validation_data=val_data`: Evaluates model performance on unseen validation data.
- Improves model generalization by tracking validation loss.

Example:
```
history = model.fit(train_data, epochs=15,
batch_size=64, validation_split=0.2)
```

Example Explanation:
- Trains for 15 epochs with a batch size of 64.
- Uses 20% of the training data for validation.
- Stores training history for later visualization of accuracy and loss.

5. Make Predictions

What is Making Predictions with an RNN?
Once trained, an RNN model can generate predictions based on new input sequences.

Syntax:
```
predictions = model.predict(test_data)
```

Syntax Explanation:

- `model.predict(test_data)`: Uses the trained model to make predictions on test data.
- Generates numerical output representing predicted values.
- Can be used for forecasting time-series data or NLP applications.

Example:

```
test_input = np.random.randn(5, 100, 1)
predictions = model.predict(test_input)
print("Predictions:", predictions)
```

Example Explanation:

- Generates predictions for five sequences, each with 100 time steps.
- Prints the predicted values, useful for evaluating model performance.

Real-Life Project: Stock Price Prediction Using LSTMs

Project Goal:

Train an LSTM model to predict future stock prices based on historical data.

Steps:

1. **Load and Preprocess Data:** Convert stock price history into sequences.
2. **Define an LSTM Model:** Use LSTM layers for long-term pattern recognition.
3. **Compile and Train the Model:** Optimize for minimal loss.
4. **Evaluate and Tune Performance:** Adjust hyperparameters based on validation loss.
5. **Make Predictions:** Forecast stock prices using the trained model.

Code Example:

```
import tensorflow as tf
import numpy as np

# Generate synthetic sequential data
x_train = np.random.randn(1000, 100, 1)  # 1000
```

```python
samples, 100 time steps, 1 feature
y_train = np.random.randn(1000, 1)

# Build LSTM model
model = tf.keras.Sequential([
    tf.keras.layers.LSTM(64, input_shape=(100, 1),
return_sequences=True),
    tf.keras.layers.LSTM(32, return_sequences=False),
    tf.keras.layers.Dense(1)
])

# Compile the model
model.compile(optimizer='adam', loss='mse')

# Train the model
model.fit(x_train, y_train, epochs=10, batch_size=32)

# Predict stock prices
x_test = np.random.randn(10, 100, 1)
predictions = model.predict(x_test)
print("Predictions:", predictions)
```

Expected Output:

```
Predictions: [[12.345], [13.678], ...]  # Simulated
future stock price predictions.
```

Chapter 32: Attention Mechanisms and Transformers in TensorFlow

Attention mechanisms and Transformer architectures have revolutionized deep learning by improving sequence modeling and parallelization. Attention allows models to focus on relevant input segments, while Transformers replace traditional recurrent layers with self-attention. TensorFlow provides built-in modules for implementing attention and Transformer models efficiently. This chapter covers key concepts, implementation, and optimization techniques for using these architectures in TensorFlow.

Key Characteristics of Attention Mechanisms and Transformers:

- **Focus on Important Input Parts:** Attention mechanisms assign different importance to different parts of the input sequence.
- **Parallel Processing:** Transformers process sequences in parallel, making training faster than RNNs.
- **Self-Attention Mechanism:** Computes relationships between all words in a sequence at once.
- **Positional Encoding:** Provides word order information, since Transformers do not use recurrence.
- **Common Architectures:** Transformer, BERT, and GPT models are widely used for NLP tasks.

Basic Rules for Implementing Attention and Transformers:

- Use `tf.keras.layers.MultiHeadAttention` for efficient multi-headed self-attention.
- Apply `PositionalEncoding` to preserve sequence order in Transformers.
- Use `LayerNormalization` to stabilize training.
- Implement attention masking to handle variable-length sequences.
- Fine-tune pre-trained Transformer models like BERT for high accuracy in NLP tasks.

Syntax Table:

SL	Function	Syntax Example	Description
1	Define Attention Layer	`tf.keras.layers.Mul tiHeadAttention(num _heads=8, key_dim=64)`	Creates a multi-headed attention layer.
2	Apply Positional Encoding	`pos_encoding = positional_encoding (sequence_length, d_model)`	Computes positional encodings for input sequences.
3	Implement Transformer Block	`TransformerBlock(nu m_heads=8, dff=512, d_model=128)`	Defines a Transformer encoder block.
4	Use Pre-Trained Transformer	`model = TFBertModel.from_pr etrained('bert-base-uncased')`	Loads a pre-trained BERT model for NLP.
5	Train Transformer Model	`model.fit(train_dat a, epochs=10, validation_data=val _data)`	Trains a Transformer model with dataset.

Syntax Explanation:

1. Define Attention Layer

What is an Attention Layer?

An attention layer allows the model to selectively focus on different input parts, improving learning for sequential data. The attention mechanism enables models to weigh different elements of the input sequence based on their importance, helping neural networks understand long-range dependencies.

Syntax:
```
import tensorflow as tf
attention_layer =
tf.keras.layers.MultiHeadAttention(num_heads=8,
key_dim=64)
```

Syntax Explanation:

- `MultiHeadAttention(num_heads=8, key_dim=64)`: Defines an attention layer with 8 attention heads.
- `key_dim=64`: Sets the dimension of key vectors for computing attention.
- Helps models learn contextual relationships between words.
- Enhances model interpretability by assigning weights to different tokens.
- Improves the ability of deep learning models to capture dependencies in long sequences.

Example:

```
output = attention_layer(query=x, value=x, key=x)
```

Example Explanation:

- Applies self-attention by using the same input as query, key, and value.
- Helps capture relationships between words in a sentence, improving translation and summarization tasks.
- Ensures better understanding of contextual meaning in NLP models.

2. Apply Positional Encoding

What is Positional Encoding?

Since Transformers lack recurrence, positional encoding provides sequence order information. This encoding method ensures that models recognize word placement within a sentence, allowing effective sequence modeling.

Syntax:

```
pos_encoding = positional_encoding(sequence_length, d_model)
```

Syntax Explanation:

- `positional_encoding(sequence_length, d_model)`: Generates sinusoidal embeddings for each token position.
- Ensures the model retains word order.
- Helps Transformers understand sequential relationships without explicit recurrence.
- Necessary for tasks like machine translation and text generation where word order matters.

Example:

```
position_embedding =
tf.keras.layers.Embedding(input_dim=1000,
output_dim=128)
```

Example Explanation:

- Creates an embedding layer to encode word positions.
- Used for maintaining order information in NLP models.
- Prevents loss of sequence structure in deep learning models.

3. Implement Transformer Block

What is a Transformer Block?

A Transformer block is a key component of Transformer models, consisting of multi-head self-attention, feed-forward layers, and normalization techniques to process sequential data efficiently.

Syntax:

```
class TransformerBlock(tf.keras.layers.Layer):
    def __init__(self, num_heads, dff, d_model):
        super(TransformerBlock, self).__init__()
        self.attention =
tf.keras.layers.MultiHeadAttention(num_heads=num_heads,
key_dim=d_model)
        self.ffn = tf.keras.Sequential([
            tf.keras.layers.Dense(dff,
activation='relu'),
            tf.keras.layers.Dense(d_model)
        ])
        self.norm1 =
```

```
tf.keras.layers.LayerNormalization(epsilon=1e-6)
        self.norm2 =
tf.keras.layers.LayerNormalization(epsilon=1e-6)

    def call(self, inputs):
        attn_output = self.attention(inputs, inputs,
inputs)
        out1 = self.norm1(inputs + attn_output)
        ffn_output = self.ffn(out1)
        return self.norm2(out1 + ffn_output)
```

Syntax Explanation:
- MultiHeadAttention(num_heads=num_heads, key_dim=d_model): Implements self-attention mechanism.
- LayerNormalization(): Stabilizes training and prevents vanishing gradients.
- Dense(dff, activation='relu'): Implements feed-forward layers with ReLU activation.
- call(self, inputs): Defines the forward pass of the Transformer block.

Example:
```
transformer_block = TransformerBlock(num_heads=8,
dff=512, d_model=128)
output = transformer_block(tf.random.uniform((1, 60,
128)))
```

Example Explanation:
- Creates a Transformer block with 8 attention heads and 512 hidden units.
- Processes an input sequence of length 60 with an embedding size of 128.
- Produces an output tensor for further processing in the Transformer model.

4. Use Pre-Trained Transformer

What is a Pre-Trained Transformer?

A pre-trained Transformer model, such as BERT or GPT, is trained on vast amounts of text data and can be fine-tuned for specific NLP tasks like classification, summarization, or translation.

Syntax:

```
from transformers import TFBertModel
bert_model = TFBertModel.from_pretrained('bert-base-uncased')
```

Syntax Explanation:

- `TFBertModel.from_pretrained('bert-base-uncased')`: Loads a BERT model pre-trained on a large text corpus.
- Allows fine-tuning on domain-specific tasks like sentiment analysis or named entity recognition.
- Enhances NLP model performance by leveraging transfer learning.

Example:

```
from transformers import BertTokenizer

tokenizer = BertTokenizer.from_pretrained('bert-base-uncased')
sample_text = "Transformers are powerful in NLP."
input_tokens = tokenizer(sample_text, return_tensors='tf')
output = bert_model(input_tokens)
```

Example Explanation:

- Tokenizes input text using a BERT tokenizer.
- Passes tokenized text through the pre-trained BERT model.
- Produces contextualized word embeddings useful for downstream tasks.

5. Train Transformer Model

What is Training a Transformer Model?
Training a Transformer model involves optimizing it for a specific task using labeled datasets. Fine-tuning pre-trained models speeds up convergence and improves performance.

Syntax:
```
model.fit(train_data, epochs=10,
validation_data=val_data)
```

Syntax Explanation:
- `train_data`: Input dataset used for training the model.
- `epochs=10`: Runs the training loop for 10 iterations.
- `validation_data=val_data`: Monitors model performance on unseen validation data.
- Helps refine model parameters for improved accuracy.

Example:
```
history = model.fit(train_data, epochs=15,
batch_size=32, validation_split=0.2)
```

Example Explanation:
- Trains the Transformer model for 15 epochs with a batch size of 32.
- Uses 20% of the training data for validation.
- Helps in tracking training progress and preventing overfitting.

Real-Life Project: Text Classification Using Transformers
Project Goal:
Train a Transformer model to classify text into different categories.
Steps:
1. **Load and Preprocess Data:** Convert text into tokenized sequences.
2. **Define Transformer Model:** Use multi-head attention layers.
3. **Compile and Train the Model:** Optimize for minimal loss.
4. **Evaluate and Tune Performance:** Adjust hyperparameters for better accuracy.
5. **Make Predictions:** Classify new text using the trained model.

Code Example:

```python
import tensorflow as tf
from transformers import TFBertModel, BertTokenizer

# Load pre-trained BERT model
tokenizer = BertTokenizer.from_pretrained('bert-base-uncased')
bert_model = TFBertModel.from_pretrained('bert-base-uncased')

# Tokenize text
sentences = ["Transformers are powerful in NLP.",
"Attention mechanism is useful."]
inputs = tokenizer(sentences, return_tensors='tf',
padding=True, truncation=True)

# Pass input through BERT
outputs = bert_model(inputs)
print(outputs.last_hidden_state.shape)
```

Expected Output:

Tensor shape representing tokenized text through BERT's encoder.

Chapter 33: Building a Language Model with TensorFlow

Language models predict the next word or sequence of words given a context. They are fundamental in Natural Language Processing (NLP) tasks such as text generation, speech recognition, and translation. TensorFlow provides tools to create, train, and fine-tune language models efficiently. This chapter explores building a language model from scratch and using pre-trained models.

Key Characteristics of Language Models:

- **Sequence Prediction:** Predicts the probability of a word following a given context.
- **Word Embeddings:** Uses embeddings to represent words numerically.
- **Recurrent and Transformer-Based Architectures:** Uses RNNs, LSTMs, or Transformers.
- **Pre-Trained Language Models:** BERT, GPT, and T5 for efficient transfer learning.
- **Application in NLP:** Used in text generation, summarization, and sentiment analysis.

Basic Rules for Implementing a Language Model:

- Use tokenization to convert text into numerical format.
- Train the model on large datasets to capture language patterns.
- Choose an appropriate architecture (RNN, LSTM, or Transformer) based on task complexity.
- Fine-tune pre-trained models to improve accuracy.
- Use attention mechanisms for better context understanding.

Syntax Table:

SL	Function	Syntax Example	Description
1	Tokenize Text	`tokenizer = tf.keras.preprocessing.text.Tokenizer()`	Converts text into tokens.

2	Create Embedding Layer	`embedding = tf.keras.layers.Emb edding(10000, 128)`	Maps words to numerical vectors.
3	Build LSTM Model	`model.add(tf.keras. layers.LSTM(128))`	Creates an LSTM-based language model.
4	Train Language Model	`model.fit(train_dat a, epochs=10)`	Trains the model on text data.
5	Generate Text	`generated_text = model.predict(input _sequence)`	Produces new text sequences.

Syntax Explanation:

1. Tokenize Text

What is Tokenization?
Tokenization is the process of converting text into numerical format by assigning unique indices to words or subwords. It is an essential preprocessing step for language models, as raw text cannot be directly processed by deep learning algorithms. Tokenization helps break down text into manageable units that can be mapped to embeddings.

Syntax:
```
import tensorflow as tf
from tensorflow.keras.preprocessing.text import
Tokenizer

tokenizer = Tokenizer(num_words=10000)
```

Syntax Explanation:
- `Tokenizer(num_words=10000)`: Creates a tokenizer that keeps only the most frequent 10,000 words.
- Converts text into token sequences.
- Helps prepare input for embedding layers in neural networks.
- Reduces vocabulary size to optimize model efficiency.
- Enables handling out-of-vocabulary words efficiently.

Example:
```
sentences = ["Language models are powerful.", "Deep
learning improves NLP."]
tokenizer.fit_on_texts(sentences)
print(tokenizer.word_index)
```

Example Explanation:
- Builds a vocabulary from the input sentences.
- Assigns unique indices to words based on frequency.
- Allows numerical representation of text data.

2. Create Embedding Layer

What is an Embedding Layer?
An embedding layer converts words into dense vector representations, capturing semantic relationships between words. Word embeddings allow the model to learn the meaning of words based on their context and relationships with other words.

Syntax:
```
embedding = tf.keras.layers.Embedding(input_dim=10000,
output_dim=128)
```

Syntax Explanation:
- `input_dim=10000`: Specifies the vocabulary size.
- `output_dim=128`: Defines the size of word vectors.
- Helps neural networks process textual data efficiently.
- Maps words into a continuous vector space.
- Reduces sparsity in text data for improved model performance.

Example:
```
model = tf.keras.Sequential([
    tf.keras.layers.Embedding(10000, 128,
input_length=100)
])
```

Example Explanation:
- Creates an embedding layer for input sequences of length 100.
- Converts tokenized words into vector representations.
- Enhances feature extraction for downstream NLP tasks.

3. Build LSTM Model
What is an LSTM Model?

A Long Short-Term Memory (LSTM) model is a specialized Recurrent Neural Network (RNN) designed to handle sequential data efficiently by mitigating the vanishing gradient problem. LSTMs maintain long-term dependencies through specialized gating mechanisms, making them ideal for text prediction and generation tasks.

Syntax:
```
model = tf.keras.Sequential([
    tf.keras.layers.Embedding(input_dim=10000,
output_dim=128, input_length=100),
    tf.keras.layers.LSTM(128, return_sequences=True),
    tf.keras.layers.LSTM(64),
    tf.keras.layers.Dense(10000, activation='softmax')
])
```

Syntax Explanation:
- `Embedding(input_dim=10000, output_dim=128, input_length=100)`: Converts word indices into dense vectors.
- `LSTM(128, return_sequences=True)`: First LSTM layer that passes sequences to the next LSTM layer.
- `LSTM(64)`: Second LSTM layer with 64 units that processes final sequence output.
- `Dense(10000, activation='softmax')`: Output layer that predicts next words in the sequence.

Example:
```
lstm_model = tf.keras.Sequential([
    tf.keras.layers.Embedding(5000, 128),
    tf.keras.layers.LSTM(100, return_sequences=True),
    tf.keras.layers.LSTM(50),
    tf.keras.layers.Dense(5000, activation='softmax')
])
```

Example Explanation:
- Creates an LSTM-based language model with two LSTM layers.
- Uses an embedding layer to convert words into vector representations.
- Outputs a probability distribution over the vocabulary for word

prediction.

4. Train Language Model

What is Training a Language Model?
Training a language model involves optimizing its parameters to learn language patterns from a dataset. The model is trained using a large corpus of text, adjusting weights through backpropagation to improve word prediction accuracy.

Syntax:
```
model.fit(train_data, epochs=10,
validation_data=val_data)
```

Syntax Explanation:
- train_data: The dataset containing text sequences for training.
- epochs=10: Specifies the number of iterations through the entire dataset.
- validation_data=val_data: Evaluates model performance on unseen data.
- Uses loss minimization techniques to refine word prediction accuracy.

Example:
```
history = model.fit(padded_sequences, np.array([[1],
[2]]), epochs=15, batch_size=32, validation_split=0.2)
```

Example Explanation:
- Trains the language model for 15 epochs using a batch size of 32.
- Uses 20% of training data for validation to monitor generalization performance.
- Stores training history for later visualization of accuracy and loss trends.

5. Generate Text

What is Text Generation?
After training, the language model can generate new sequences of text by predicting the most probable next words based on an initial input sequence.

Syntax:
```
predicted_text = model.predict(input_sequence)
```

Syntax Explanation:
- `model.predict(input_sequence)`: Uses the trained model to generate text based on input data.
- Outputs a sequence of word probabilities that can be converted to readable text.
- Allows for creative applications such as chatbot responses or automatic story writing.

Example:
```
seed_text = "Deep learning models are"
encoded_sequence =
tokenizer.texts_to_sequences([seed_text])
padded_sequence = pad_sequences(encoded_sequence,
maxlen=10, padding='post')
prediction = model.predict(padded_sequence)
predicted_word =
tokenizer.index_word[np.argmax(prediction)]
print(seed_text, predicted_word)
```

Example Explanation:
- Converts seed text into a numerical sequence using a trained tokenizer.
- Pads sequence to match input size required by the model.
- Predicts the next word and prints the generated text output.

Real-Life Project: Text Generation Using LSTM
Project Goal:
Train an LSTM-based language model to generate coherent text based on input sequences. The model learns the structure of the text and generates contextually relevant sequences.

Steps:

1. **Load and Preprocess Data:** Tokenize and convert text to sequences.
2. **Build the LSTM Model:** Use an embedding layer followed by LSTM layers.
3. **Compile and Train the Model:** Optimize using categorical cross-entropy loss.
4. **Generate Text:** Predict new sequences using the trained model.
5. **Evaluate and Tune Performance:** Adjust hyperparameters for better output.

Code Example:

```
import tensorflow as tf
import numpy as np

# Sample dataset
sentences = ["TensorFlow makes language modeling
easy.", "Recurrent models capture sequence patterns."]

# Tokenization
tokenizer = tf.keras.preprocessing.text.Tokenizer()
tokenizer.fit_on_texts(sentences)
sequences = tokenizer.texts_to_sequences(sentences)

# Padding
from tensorflow.keras.preprocessing.sequence import
pad_sequences
padded_sequences = pad_sequences(sequences, maxlen=10,
padding='post')

# Build LSTM model
model = tf.keras.Sequential([
    tf.keras.layers.Embedding(input_dim=10000,
output_dim=128, input_length=10),
    tf.keras.layers.LSTM(128, return_sequences=True),
    tf.keras.layers.LSTM(64),
```

```python
    tf.keras.layers.Dense(10000, activation='softmax')
])

# Compile model
model.compile(optimizer='adam',
loss='sparse_categorical_crossentropy',
metrics=['accuracy'])

# Train model
model.fit(padded_sequences, np.array([[1], [2]]),
epochs=10)
```

Expected Output:

Training logs showing loss and accuracy improvements.

Chapter 34: Sentiment Analysis and Text Classification in TensorFlow

Sentiment analysis and text classification are key applications of Natural Language Processing (NLP), enabling models to classify text into categories such as positive or negative sentiment, spam detection, and topic classification. TensorFlow provides powerful tools such as embedding layers, LSTMs, and Transformers to build and train text classifiers efficiently.

Key Characteristics of Sentiment Analysis and Text Classification:

- **Supervised Learning Task:** Requires labeled data for training.
- **Text Preprocessing:** Tokenization, padding, and vectorization are essential.
- **Word Embeddings:** Transforms words into dense vector representations.
- **Deep Learning Architectures:** Uses CNNs, RNNs, LSTMs, and Transformers.
- **Fine-Tuning Pre-Trained Models:** BERT and GPT improve classification accuracy.

Basic Rules for Implementing Text Classification:

- Use TextVectorization or Tokenizer for efficient text tokenization.
- Convert words into embeddings using Embedding layers or pre-trained word vectors.
- Choose an appropriate model architecture based on dataset complexity.
- Apply dropout and batch normalization to prevent overfitting.
- Evaluate models using accuracy, precision, recall, and F1-score.

Syntax Table:

SL	Function	Syntax Example	Description
1	Tokenize Text	`tokenizer = tf.keras.preprocessing.text.Tokenizer()`	Converts text into token sequences.
2	Vectorize Text Using Embedding	`embedding = tf.keras.layers.Embedding(10000, 128)`	Maps words to numerical vectors.
3	Define LSTM Model	`model.add(tf.keras.layers.LSTM(128))`	Creates an LSTM-based classifier.
4	Train Classification Model	`model.fit(train_data, epochs=10, validation_data=val_data)`	Trains the model for text classification.
5	Evaluate Model Performance	`model.evaluate(test_data)`	Computes accuracy and loss on test data.

Syntax Explanation:

1. Tokenize Text

What is Tokenization?

Tokenization is the process of converting raw text into numerical format by assigning indices to words. It is a fundamental preprocessing step for deep learning models.

Syntax:

```
import tensorflow as tf
from tensorflow.keras.preprocessing.text import Tokenizer
tokenizer = Tokenizer(num_words=10000, oov_token="<OOV>")
```

Syntax Explanation:

- `Tokenizer(num_words=10000)`: Keeps the most frequent 10,000 words.
- `oov_token="<OOV>"`: Handles out-of-vocabulary words.
- Converts text into sequences for model training.

Example:
```
sentences = ["I love this product!", "This movie was
terrible."]
tokenizer.fit_on_texts(sentences)
print(tokenizer.word_index)
```

Example Explanation:
- Assigns unique indices to words in the input text.
- Prepares text for embedding layers and deep learning models.

2. Vectorize Text Using Embedding

What is an Embedding Layer?
An embedding layer transforms tokenized words into dense vectors that capture semantic relationships.

Syntax:
```
embedding = tf.keras.layers.Embedding(input_dim=10000,
output_dim=128)
```

Syntax Explanation:
- input_dim=10000: Vocabulary size.
- output_dim=128: Size of the word vectors.
- Converts discrete words into meaningful numerical representations.

Example:
```
model = tf.keras.Sequential([
    tf.keras.layers.Embedding(10000, 128,
input_length=100)
])
```

Example Explanation:
- Creates an embedding layer for input sequences of length 100.
- Helps neural networks process textual data efficiently.

3. Define LSTM Model

What is an LSTM Model?

A Long Short-Term Memory (LSTM) model is a specialized type of Recurrent Neural Network (RNN) designed to capture long-term dependencies in sequential data. It consists of memory cells that retain important information over time and gates that regulate the flow of data.

Syntax:

```
model = tf.keras.Sequential([
    tf.keras.layers.Embedding(input_dim=10000,
output_dim=128, input_length=100),
    tf.keras.layers.LSTM(128, return_sequences=True),
    tf.keras.layers.LSTM(64),
    tf.keras.layers.Dense(1, activation='sigmoid')
])
```

Syntax Explanation:

- Embedding(10000, 128): Converts words into dense vector representations.
- LSTM(128, return_sequences=True): First LSTM layer that returns sequences to the next LSTM layer.
- LSTM(64): Second LSTM layer that processes the final sequence output.
- Dense(1, activation='sigmoid'): Output layer that classifies input as positive or negative.

Example:

```
lstm_model = tf.keras.Sequential([
    tf.keras.layers.Embedding(5000, 128),
    tf.keras.layers.LSTM(100, return_sequences=True),
    tf.keras.layers.LSTM(50),
    tf.keras.layers.Dense(1, activation='sigmoid')
])
```

Example Explanation:

- Builds an LSTM-based sentiment classifier.
- Uses two LSTM layers for sequential pattern learning.
- Outputs a single probability score for classification.

4. Train Classification Model

What is Training a Classification Model?
Training a classification model involves optimizing model weights using labeled training data to minimize error and improve prediction accuracy.
Syntax:
```
model.fit(train_data, train_labels, epochs=10,
validation_data=(val_data, val_labels))
```

Syntax Explanation:
- `train_data, train_labels`: The dataset and corresponding labels for training.
- `epochs=10`: Runs training for 10 iterations over the dataset.
- `validation_data=(val_data, val_labels)`: Evaluates model performance on unseen data.
- Helps adjust model parameters for better classification accuracy.

Example:
```
history = model.fit(padded_sequences, labels,
epochs=15, batch_size=32, validation_split=0.2)
```

Example Explanation:
- Trains the model for 15 epochs using mini-batches of size 32.
- Splits 20% of data for validation to monitor performance.
- Stores training history for later analysis.

5. Evaluate Model Performance

What is Model Evaluation?
Evaluating a model assesses its ability to classify unseen data correctly using metrics such as accuracy, precision, recall, and loss.
Syntax:
```
loss, accuracy = model.evaluate(test_data, test_labels)
```
Syntax Explanation:
- `model.evaluate(test_data, test_labels)`: Computes the loss and accuracy on test data.
- Helps determine model generalization to new inputs.

- Guides hyperparameter tuning for better results.

Example:

```
test_loss, test_accuracy =
model.evaluate(test_sequences, test_labels)
print(f"Test Accuracy: {test_accuracy:.2f}")
```

Example Explanation:
- Evaluates the model on test sequences and labels.
- Prints the test accuracy to measure model effectiveness.
- Helps identify potential overfitting or underfitting issues.

Real-Life Project: Sentiment Analysis of Movie Reviews
Project Goal:
Train an LSTM-based sentiment analysis model to classify movie reviews as positive or negative.
Steps:
1. **Load and Preprocess Data:** Tokenize and convert text to sequences.
2. **Build the LSTM Model:** Use an embedding layer followed by LSTM layers.
3. **Compile and Train the Model:** Optimize using binary cross-entropy loss.
4. **Evaluate and Tune Performance:** Use accuracy, precision, and recall metrics.
5. **Make Predictions:** Classify new reviews using the trained model.

Code Example:

```
import tensorflow as tf
import numpy as np

# Sample dataset
sentences = ["The movie was fantastic!", "I hated the
storyline."]
labels = np.array([1, 0])  # 1 = Positive, 0 = Negative

# Tokenization
```

```python
tokenizer = tf.keras.preprocessing.text.Tokenizer()
tokenizer.fit_on_texts(sentences)
sequences = tokenizer.texts_to_sequences(sentences)

# Padding
from tensorflow.keras.preprocessing.sequence import
pad_sequences
padded_sequences = pad_sequences(sequences, maxlen=10,
padding='post')

# Build LSTM model
model = tf.keras.Sequential([
    tf.keras.layers.Embedding(input_dim=10000,
output_dim=128, input_length=10),
    tf.keras.layers.LSTM(128, return_sequences=True),
    tf.keras.layers.LSTM(64),
    tf.keras.layers.Dense(1, activation='sigmoid')
])

# Compile model
model.compile(optimizer='adam',
loss='binary_crossentropy', metrics=['accuracy'])

# Train model
model.fit(padded_sequences, labels, epochs=10)
```

Expected Output:

Training logs showing accuracy and loss improvements.

Chapter 35: Machine Translation with TensorFlow

Machine translation is a fundamental Natural Language Processing (NLP) task that involves automatically translating text from one language to another. TensorFlow provides powerful tools like sequence-to-sequence (Seq2Seq) models, attention mechanisms, and Transformers to build and train robust translation models. This chapter explores how to build a machine translation system from scratch using TensorFlow.

Key Characteristics of Machine Translation:

- **Sequence-to-Sequence Learning:** Uses an encoder-decoder architecture for language conversion.
- **Tokenization and Embeddings:** Converts words into numerical representations for processing.
- **Recurrent and Transformer-Based Architectures:** Uses RNNs, LSTMs, or Transformers.
- **Attention Mechanisms:** Helps the model focus on relevant words during translation.
- **Pre-Trained Models:** BERT and T5 improve translation accuracy.

Basic Rules for Implementing Machine Translation:

- Use TextVectorization or Tokenizer for efficient text tokenization.
- Convert words into embeddings using Embedding layers or pre-trained word vectors.
- Choose an appropriate sequence-to-sequence model based on dataset complexity.
- Apply attention mechanisms for improved translation accuracy.
- Fine-tune Transformer models like T5 for better performance.

Syntax Table:

SL	Function	Syntax Example	Description
1	Tokenize Text	`tokenizer = tf.keras.preprocessing.text.Tokenizer()`	Converts text into token sequences.

2	Define Embedding Layer	`embedding = tf.keras.layers.Embedding(10000, 128)`	Maps words to numerical vectors.
3	Define Encoder-Decoder Model	`encoder = tf.keras.layers.LSTM(128, return_sequences=True)`	Creates an LSTM-based encoder.
4	Train Translation Model	`model.fit(train_data, epochs=10, validation_data=val_data)`	Trains the Seq2Seq translation model.
5	Make Translation Predictions	`translated_text = model.predict(input_sequence)`	Generates translated text sequences.

Syntax Explanation:

1. Tokenize Text

What is Tokenization?
Tokenization is the process of converting text into numerical format by assigning unique indices to words. It is an essential preprocessing step for training machine translation models. Tokenization helps break down sentences into smaller, meaningful units, allowing the model to learn word dependencies and semantic structures.

Syntax:
```
import tensorflow as tf
from tensorflow.keras.preprocessing.text import Tokenizer

tokenizer = Tokenizer(num_words=10000, oov_token="<OOV>")
```

Syntax Explanation:
- `Tokenizer(num_words=10000)`: Keeps the most frequent 10,000 words in the vocabulary.
- `oov_token="<OOV>"`: Replaces unknown words with a special

token <OOV> to handle out-of-vocabulary words.

- Converts input text into integer sequences for deep learning models.
- Reduces memory usage and improves model efficiency by limiting vocabulary size.
- Ensures consistency in text preprocessing across training and inference.

Example:
```
sentences = ["Bonjour, comment ça va?", "Hello, how are you?"]
tokenizer.fit_on_texts(sentences)
print(tokenizer.word_index)
```

Example Explanation:
- Builds a vocabulary dictionary mapping words to unique indices.
- Prepares text data for embedding and deep learning models.
- Ensures consistency in representing different language tokens.

2. Define Embedding Layer

What is an Embedding Layer?
An embedding layer transforms tokenized words into dense vectors that capture semantic relationships between words. It helps models learn contextual meanings and improves translation quality by mapping words into a high-dimensional space.

Syntax:
```
embedding = tf.keras.layers.Embedding(input_dim=10000,
output_dim=128)
```

Syntax Explanation:
- input_dim=10000: Defines the total vocabulary size.
- output_dim=128: Specifies the size of word embeddings (vector dimensions).
- Maps discrete words into continuous vector spaces for better generalization.

- Helps capture similarities between semantically related words.
- Essential for deep learning models processing text data.

Example:
```
model = tf.keras.Sequential([
    tf.keras.layers.Embedding(10000, 128,
input_length=100)
])
```

Example Explanation:
- Initializes an embedding layer for text inputs.
- Assigns a 128-dimensional vector representation to each word.
- Allows model to process input sentences with a maximum length of 100.

3. Define Encoder-Decoder Model

What is an Encoder-Decoder Model?

An encoder-decoder model is a sequence-to-sequence (Seq2Seq) architecture used for transforming input sequences into output sequences of varying lengths. It consists of an encoder that processes the input and a decoder that generates the output, making it ideal for translation tasks.

Syntax:
```
encoder_inputs = tf.keras.layers.Input(shape=(10,))
embedding = tf.keras.layers.Embedding(input_dim=10000,
output_dim=128)(encoder_inputs)
encoder_lstm = tf.keras.layers.LSTM(128,
return_sequences=True, return_state=True)
encoder_outputs, state_h, state_c =
encoder_lstm(embedding)

decoder_inputs = tf.keras.layers.Input(shape=(10,))
decoder_embedding =
tf.keras.layers.Embedding(input_dim=10000,
output_dim=128)(decoder_inputs)
decoder_lstm = tf.keras.layers.LSTM(128,
return_sequences=True, return_state=True)
decoder_outputs, _, _ = decoder_lstm(decoder_embedding,
initial_state=[state_h, state_c])
```

Syntax Explanation:

- `encoder_inputs`: Defines the input layer for the encoder.
- `Embedding(10000, 128)`: Converts words into dense vector representations.
- `LSTM(128, return_state=True)`: Stores the hidden and cell states for the decoder.
- `decoder_inputs`: Defines the input layer for the decoder.
- Uses the final hidden states of the encoder as the initial states for the decoder.

Example:

```
encoder_inputs = tf.keras.layers.Input(shape=(None,))
embedding = tf.keras.layers.Embedding(input_dim=10000,
output_dim=256)(encoder_inputs)
encoder_lstm = tf.keras.layers.LSTM(256,
return_state=True)
encoder_outputs, state_h, state_c =
encoder_lstm(embedding)
```

Example Explanation:

- Defines an encoder with a larger embedding and LSTM size.
- Captures more complex sentence structures for translation.
- Stores state vectors for the decoder to generate the target sentence.

4. Train Translation Model

What is Training a Translation Model?

Training a translation model involves optimizing the parameters of an encoder-decoder network to minimize the difference between predicted and actual translations. It requires backpropagation through time (BPTT) and sequence alignment.

Syntax:

```
model.compile(optimizer='adam',
loss='sparse_categorical_crossentropy',
metrics=['accuracy'])
model.fit([train_input, train_target],
```

```
train_target_labels, epochs=10, batch_size=32,
validation_split=0.2)
```

Syntax Explanation:
- `optimizer='adam'`: Uses the Adam optimizer for stable convergence.
- `loss='sparse_categorical_crossentropy'`: Applies categorical cross-entropy loss for multi-class classification.
- `metrics=['accuracy']`: Tracks accuracy during training.
- `train_input, train_target`: Input and target sequences for training.
- `epochs=10`: Trains the model for 10 iterations over the dataset.
- `batch_size=32`: Processes 32 samples per training step.

Example:
```
history = model.fit([train_sequences,
target_sequences], target_labels, epochs=15,
batch_size=64, validation_data=(val_input, val_target))
```

Example Explanation:
- Trains for 15 epochs using larger batch sizes for efficiency.
- Uses a validation set to monitor performance and prevent overfitting.
- Stores training history for plotting accuracy and loss curves.

5. Make Translation Predictions

What is Making Translation Predictions?
Once trained, the model can generate translated sequences by feeding an input sentence into the encoder and using the decoder to predict each word in the output sentence step by step.

Syntax:
```
translated_text = model.predict(input_sequence)
```

Syntax Explanation:
- `model.predict(input_sequence)`: Uses the trained model to generate a translated sequence.
- Outputs a sequence of probability distributions over the

vocabulary.

- Requires post-processing to convert token indices into human-readable words.

Example:
```
input_text = "Bonjour, comment ça va?"
input_seq =
tokenizer_fr.texts_to_sequences([input_text])
input_padded = pad_sequences(input_seq, maxlen=10,
padding='post')
predicted_seq = model.predict([input_padded,
np.zeros((1, 10))])
predicted_text =
tokenizer_en.sequences_to_texts(predicted_seq)
print(predicted_text)
```

Example Explanation:
- Converts French input text into a tokenized sequence.
- Pads the sequence to match model input length.
- Uses the trained model to predict the English translation.
- Converts the predicted sequence back to text using the English tokenizer.

Real-Life Project: French to English Translation
Project Goal:
Train a sequence-to-sequence (Seq2Seq) model to translate French sentences into English.
Steps:
1. **Load and Preprocess Data:** Tokenize and convert text to sequences.
2. **Build an Encoder-Decoder Model:** Use embedding, LSTM layers, and attention.
3. **Compile and Train the Model:** Optimize using categorical cross-entropy loss.
4. **Evaluate and Tune Performance:** Use BLEU score to measure translation quality.
5. **Make Predictions:** Translate new French sentences using the

trained model.

Code Example:

```python
import tensorflow as tf
import numpy as np

# Sample dataset
french_sentences = ["Bonjour, comment ça va?", "Je suis
content de te voir"]
english_sentences = ["Hello, how are you?", "I am happy
to see you"]

# Tokenization
tokenizer_fr = tf.keras.preprocessing.text.Tokenizer()
tokenizer_en = tf.keras.preprocessing.text.Tokenizer()
tokenizer_fr.fit_on_texts(french_sentences)
tokenizer_en.fit_on_texts(english_sentences)

fr_sequences =
tokenizer_fr.texts_to_sequences(french_sentences)
en_sequences =
tokenizer_en.texts_to_sequences(english_sentences)

# Padding
from tensorflow.keras.preprocessing.sequence import
pad_sequences
fr_padded = pad_sequences(fr_sequences, maxlen=10,
padding='post')
en_padded = pad_sequences(en_sequences, maxlen=10,
padding='post')

# Build Seq2Seq Model
encoder_inputs = tf.keras.layers.Input(shape=(10,))
embedding = tf.keras.layers.Embedding(input_dim=10000,
output_dim=128)(encoder_inputs)
encoder_lstm = tf.keras.layers.LSTM(128,
return_sequences=True, return_state=True)
```

```
encoder_outputs, state_h, state_c =
encoder_lstm(embedding)

decoder_inputs = tf.keras.layers.Input(shape=(10,))
decoder_embedding =
tf.keras.layers.Embedding(input_dim=10000,
output_dim=128)(decoder_inputs)
decoder_lstm = tf.keras.layers.LSTM(128,
return_sequences=True, return_state=True)
decoder_outputs, _, _ = decoder_lstm(decoder_embedding,
initial_state=[state_h, state_c])

output_layer = tf.keras.layers.Dense(10000,
activation='softmax')
decoder_outputs = output_layer(decoder_outputs)

model = tf.keras.Model([encoder_inputs,
decoder_inputs], decoder_outputs)

# Compile model
model.compile(optimizer='adam',
loss='sparse_categorical_crossentropy',
metrics=['accuracy'])

# Train model
model.fit([fr_padded, en_padded], np.array(en_padded),
epochs=10)
```

Expected Output:

Training logs showing loss and accuracy improvements.

Chapter 36: Time Series Forecasting with TensorFlow

Time series forecasting is a critical application of deep learning used to predict future values based on past data. TensorFlow provides powerful tools such as LSTMs, GRUs, and CNNs for analyzing sequential data. This chapter explores time series modeling techniques using TensorFlow, including preprocessing, model selection, and evaluation.

Key Characteristics of Time Series Forecasting:

- **Sequential Data Dependency:** Predicts future values based on past observations.
- **Feature Engineering:** Time-based features such as trend, seasonality, and cyclic patterns are important.
- **Long Short-Term Memory (LSTM) Networks:** Captures long-range dependencies in sequential data.
- **Sliding Window Techniques:** Creates input-output pairs from past observations.
- **Evaluation Metrics:** Mean Absolute Error (MAE) and Root Mean Squared Error (RMSE) are used for model performance assessment.

Basic Rules for Implementing Time Series Forecasting:

- Use proper scaling techniques to normalize data.
- Split data into training, validation, and test sets to prevent data leakage.
- Choose an appropriate window size for sequence modeling.
- Select the right architecture, such as LSTMs, GRUs, or Transformers.
- Evaluate performance using time series-specific metrics.

Syntax Table:

SL	Function	Syntax Example	Description
1	Load Time Series Data	`data = pd.read_csv('time _series.csv')`	Loads a time series dataset.

2	Normalize Data	`scaler = MinMaxScaler().fit(data)`	Scales data for better model convergence.
3	Define LSTM Model	`model.add(tf.keras.layers.LSTM(64))`	Builds an LSTM-based forecasting model.
4	Train Forecasting Model	`model.fit(train_data, epochs=10)`	Trains the model on time series data.
5	Make Forecast Predictions	`predictions = model.predict(test_data)`	Generates future predictions.

Syntax Explanation:

1. Load Time Series Data

What is Time Series Data Loading?
Loading time series data is the first step in forecasting, involving retrieving data from a source and organizing it into a structured format for analysis.
Syntax:
```
import pandas as pd

data = pd.read_csv('time_series.csv',
parse_dates=['date'], index_col='date')
```

Syntax Explanation:
- `pd.read_csv('time_series.csv')`: Reads the dataset from a CSV file.
- `parse_dates=['date']`: Ensures that the date column is parsed correctly.
- `index_col='date'`: Sets the date column as the index for time-based operations.

Example:
```
print(data.head())
```

Example Explanation:

- Displays the first five rows of the dataset.
- Ensures that the time series data is loaded correctly.

2. Normalize Data

What is Data Normalization?

Normalization scales numeric values to a specific range, improving training stability and convergence speed.

Syntax:

```
from sklearn.preprocessing import MinMaxScaler

scaler = MinMaxScaler()
data_scaled = scaler.fit_transform(data)
```

Syntax Explanation:

- `MinMaxScaler()`: Scales values between 0 and 1 to standardize input data.
- `fit_transform(data)`: Fits the scaler to data and transforms it accordingly.

Example:

```
scaled_df = pd.DataFrame(data_scaled,
columns=data.columns, index=data.index)
```

Example Explanation:

- Converts the scaled data back into a DataFrame.
- Preserves the original time index for analysis.

3. Create Windowed Dataset

What is a Windowed Dataset?

A windowed dataset transforms time series data into overlapping sequences of input-output pairs. This technique enables models to learn patterns and trends from past data, making accurate future predictions possible.

Syntax:
```python
def create_windowed_dataset(data, window_size):
    sequences = []
    targets = []
    for i in range(len(data) - window_size):

sequences.append(data.iloc[i:i+window_size].values)
        targets.append(data.iloc[i+window_size].values)
    return np.array(sequences), np.array(targets)
```

Syntax Explanation:
- window_size: Defines the number of past time steps used for prediction.
- Iterates through the dataset to extract input (sequences) and corresponding target (targets).
- Converts structured sequences into NumPy arrays for model compatibility.

Example:
```python
window_size = 20
X, y = create_windowed_dataset(data, window_size)
```

Example Explanation:
- Creates input-output pairs for time series forecasting.
- Ensures that past data contributes to predicting future values.

4. Define LSTM Model

What is an LSTM Model for Time Series?
Long Short-Term Memory (LSTM) networks are well-suited for time series forecasting due to their ability to capture long-range dependencies and learn temporal patterns.

Syntax:
```python
model = tf.keras.Sequential([
    tf.keras.layers.LSTM(64, return_sequences=True,
input_shape=(window_size, 1)),
    tf.keras.layers.LSTM(32, return_sequences=False),
    tf.keras.layers.Dense(1)
])
```

Syntax Explanation:

- `LSTM(64, return_sequences=True)`: First LSTM layer that returns all time steps.
- `LSTM(32, return_sequences=False)`: Second LSTM layer that outputs the final state.
- `Dense(1)`: Fully connected layer for output prediction.
- `input_shape=(window_size, 1)`: Defines the input format.

Example:

```
lstm_model = tf.keras.Sequential([
    tf.keras.layers.LSTM(50, return_sequences=True,
input_shape=(30, 1)),
    tf.keras.layers.LSTM(25),
    tf.keras.layers.Dense(1)
])
```

Example Explanation:

- Uses two LSTM layers to capture long-term dependencies.
- Processes input sequences of length 30.
- Outputs a single forecasted value per time step.

5. Train Time Series Model

What is Training a Time Series Model?

Training a time series model involves optimizing model weights to minimize prediction error using historical data.

Syntax:

```
model.compile(optimizer='adam', loss='mse')
model.fit(X_train, y_train, epochs=10, batch_size=16,
validation_data=(X_test, y_test))
```

Syntax Explanation:

- `optimizer='adam'`: Uses the Adam optimizer for adaptive learning rate control.
- `loss='mse'`: Uses Mean Squared Error as the loss function.
- `epochs=10`: Trains for 10 iterations over the dataset.

- `batch_size=16`: Processes 16 samples per training step.
- `validation_data`: Evaluates model performance on unseen data.

Example:
```
history = model.fit(X_train, y_train, epochs=20,
batch_size=32, validation_split=0.2)
```

Example Explanation:
- Trains the model for 20 epochs.
- Uses a batch size of 32 for efficiency.
- Splits 20% of training data for validation.
- Tracks loss trends to prevent overfitting.

Real-Life Project: Predicting Stock Prices

Project Goal:

Train an LSTM-based model to predict future stock prices using historical data.

Steps:
1. **Load and Preprocess Data:** Normalize and structure time series data.
2. **Create Sliding Windows:** Generate input-output pairs for sequence learning.
3. **Build the LSTM Model:** Use an LSTM layer followed by dense layers.
4. **Compile and Train the Model:** Optimize using mean squared error (MSE).
5. **Evaluate and Forecast:** Measure performance and make predictions.

Code Example:

```
import tensorflow as tf
import numpy as np

# Generate synthetic time series data
timestamps = np.arange(1000)
```

```python
data_values = np.sin(0.01 * timestamps) +
np.random.normal(scale=0.1, size=1000)

data = pd.DataFrame({'timestamp': timestamps, 'value':
data_values})
data['timestamp'] = pd.to_datetime(data['timestamp'],
unit='s')
data.set_index('timestamp', inplace=True)

# Normalize data
scaler = MinMaxScaler()
data['value'] = scaler.fit_transform(data[['value']])

# Create sequences
def create_sequences(data, window_size):
    sequences = []
    targets = []
    for i in range(len(data) - window_size):

sequences.append(data.iloc[i:i+window_size].values)
        targets.append(data.iloc[i+window_size].values)
    return np.array(sequences), np.array(targets)

window_size = 20
X, y = create_sequences(data, window_size)
X_train, X_test, y_train, y_test = X[:800], X[800:],
y[:800], y[800:]

# Build LSTM Model
model = tf.keras.Sequential([
    tf.keras.layers.LSTM(64, return_sequences=True,
input_shape=(window_size, 1)),
    tf.keras.layers.LSTM(32, return_sequences=False),
    tf.keras.layers.Dense(1)
])

# Compile model
```

```python
model.compile(optimizer='adam', loss='mse')

# Train model
model.fit(X_train, y_train, epochs=10, batch_size=16,
validation_data=(X_test, y_test))
```

Expected Output:

```
Training logs showing loss reduction over epochs.
```

Chapter 37: Reinforcement Learning with TensorFlow

Reinforcement Learning (RL) is a machine learning paradigm where an agent learns by interacting with an environment to maximize cumulative rewards. TensorFlow provides powerful tools such as TensorFlow Agents (TF-Agents) to implement and train RL models. This chapter explores key concepts of RL, environment setup, policy learning, and model training using TensorFlow.

Key Characteristics of Reinforcement Learning:

- **Agent-Environment Interaction:** The agent learns by interacting with an environment.
- **Reward-Based Learning:** The agent maximizes cumulative rewards over time.
- **Markov Decision Process (MDP):** Models decision-making problems using states, actions, and rewards.
- **Policy and Value Functions:** Defines strategies for selecting actions.
- **Exploration vs. Exploitation Trade-off:** Balances exploring new actions and exploiting known ones.

Basic Rules for Implementing Reinforcement Learning:

- Define an environment using OpenAI Gym or custom environments.
- Choose an appropriate RL algorithm (e.g., Q-learning, DDPG, PPO, A3C).
- Design a reward function that aligns with the learning goal.
- Implement an agent to learn optimal policies using neural networks.
- Train and evaluate the model based on performance metrics like average reward.

Syntax Table:

SL	Function	Syntax Example	Description
1	Create RL Environment	`env = gym.make('CartPole-v1')`	Loads a predefined reinforcement learning environment.
2	Define RL Agent	`agent = tf_agents.agents.DqnAgent(...)`	Creates a reinforcement learning agent.
3	Train RL Model	`agent.train(learning_data)`	Trains the RL model using collected experiences.
4	Evaluate RL Model	`agent.evaluate(environment)`	Assesses the model's performance on test data.
5	Deploy and Run RL Agent	`action = agent.policy.action(state)`	Executes an action using the trained policy.

Syntax Explanation:

1. Create RL Environment

What is an RL Environment?

A reinforcement learning environment provides a controlled setting where an agent can take actions and receive rewards, essential for training RL models. The environment acts as the problem space in which the agent learns optimal behaviors through trial and error. Environments can be real-world simulations or predefined benchmarks such as OpenAI Gym.

Syntax:

```
import gym

env = gym.make('CartPole-v1')
env.reset()
```

Syntax Explanation:

- `gym.make('CartPole-v1')`: Loads the CartPole environment, a common benchmark for RL models.
- `env.reset()`: Initializes the environment before training begins.
- Provides the agent with an initial state to start interacting with.
- Used to ensure that the simulation starts fresh at the beginning of each episode.

Example:

```
state = env.reset()
print("Initial State:", state)
```

Example Explanation:

- Outputs the initial state representation of the environment.
- Helps verify the setup before training an agent.
- Ensures the model can properly interact with the environment.

2. Define RL Agent

What is an RL Agent?

An RL agent interacts with the environment, taking actions and learning policies to maximize rewards. The agent learns a decision-making strategy based on state observations and feedback signals, gradually improving its policy over time.

Syntax:

```
from tf_agents.agents.dqn import dqn_agent
agent = dqn_agent.DqnAgent(time_step_spec, action_spec,
q_network, optimizer)
```

Syntax Explanation:

- `DqnAgent(...)`: Implements a Deep Q-Network (DQN) agent for RL.
- `time_step_spec`: Defines the time step specifications, including state observations.
- `action_spec`: Specifies valid actions the agent can take.
- `q_network`: A neural network that estimates the value of actions.
- `optimizer`: An optimization algorithm to improve the learning process.

Example:
```
from tf_agents.networks.q_network import QNetwork

q_network = QNetwork(env.observation_space.shape,
env.action_space.n)
agent = dqn_agent.DqnAgent(time_step_spec, action_spec,
q_network, optimizer)
```

Example Explanation:
- Creates a Q-network that maps state inputs to action-value estimates.
- Initializes a DQN agent with this network.
- The agent learns to select optimal actions over time.

3. Train RL Model

What is Training an RL Model?
Training a reinforcement learning model involves improving the agent's ability to maximize cumulative rewards over time by interacting with an environment. The training process uses an exploration-exploitation strategy where the agent learns from both trial-and-error actions and previous experiences.

Syntax:
```
agent.train(learning_data)
```

Syntax Explanation:
- `agent.train(learning_data)`: Trains the RL model by optimizing its policy over multiple iterations.
- Uses a reinforcement learning algorithm like DQN, PPO, or A3C.
- Gradually refines action-selection strategies by adjusting Q-values.
- Stores past experiences in replay buffers to prevent catastrophic forgetting.
- Incorporates exploration techniques like epsilon-greedy strategies to balance learning.

Example:
```
num_iterations = 5000
for i in range(num_iterations):
    experience = collect_experience(env, agent)
    agent.train(experience)
```

Example Explanation:
- Runs training for 5000 iterations.
- Collects experiences by interacting with the environment.
- Uses experience replay to update the model efficiently.

4. Evaluate RL Model

What is Evaluating an RL Model?
Evaluation measures how well the trained RL agent performs in the environment by testing its learned policy without exploration.
Syntax:
```
agent.evaluate(environment)
```
Syntax Explanation:
- `agent.evaluate(environment)`: Runs the trained model on test data to measure performance.
- Ensures the model generalizes well across various states.
- Assesses stability in action selection and decision-making.
- Helps fine-tune hyperparameters like learning rate and discount factor.

Example:
```
total_reward = 0
for episode in range(10):
    state = env.reset()
    episode_reward = 0
    while not state.is_last():
        action = agent.policy.action(state)
        state = env.step(action.action)
        episode_reward += state.reward.numpy()
    total_reward += episode_reward
print("Average Reward over 10 episodes:", total_reward
/ 10)
```

Example Explanation:

- Runs 10 test episodes to compute the average reward.
- Measures the effectiveness of the trained agent's policy.
- Helps compare different RL models and training strategies.

5. Deploy and Run RL Agent

What is Deploying an RL Agent?

Deployment involves running the trained reinforcement learning model in a live environment where it makes real-time decisions based on observed states.

Syntax:

```
action = agent.policy.action(state)
```

Syntax Explanation:

- `agent.policy.action(state)`: Uses the trained policy to select an optimal action.
- Runs in real-world simulations or production applications.
- Can be integrated into robotics, gaming, or automated trading.

Example:

```
state = env.reset()
while not state.is_last():
    action = agent.policy.action(state)
    state = env.step(action.action)
    print("Action Taken:", action.action.numpy())
```

Example Explanation:

- Resets the environment to the initial state.
- Executes actions in real-time based on the trained policy.
- Demonstrates the RL model making autonomous decisions in its environment.

Real-Life Project: Training an RL Agent for CartPole Balancing
Project Goal:

Train an RL agent to balance a pole on a cart using reinforcement learning techniques.

Steps:

1. **Set Up the Environment:** Load the CartPole environment from OpenAl Gym.
2. **Define the RL Agent:** Use a DQN agent to learn optimal balancing policies.
3. **Train the Agent:** Optimize the model to maximize reward.
4. **Evaluate Performance:** Measure the agent's success in keeping the pole balanced.
5. **Deploy and Test:** Run the trained agent in the environment.

Code Example:

```python
import tensorflow as tf
import gym
import numpy as np
from tf_agents.environments import suite_gym
from tf_agents.agents.dqn import dqn_agent
from tf_agents.networks.q_network import QNetwork
from tf_agents.trajectories import time_step as ts
from tf_agents.replay_buffers import
tf_uniform_replay_buffer


# Load environment
env = suite_gym.load('CartPole-v1')
time_step_spec =
ts.time_step_spec(env.observation_spec())
action_spec = env.action_spec()


# Define Q-Network
q_network = QNetwork(env.observation_spec(),
env.action_spec().maximum + 1)


# Define DQN Agent
agent = dqn_agent.DqnAgent(
    time_step_spec,
    action_spec,
    q_network=q_network,
```

```python
    optimizer=tf.keras.optimizers.Adam(learning_rate=1e-3),

    td_errors_loss_fn=tf.keras.losses.Huber(reduction="none
")
)
agent.initialize()

# Training loop
num_iterations = 10000
total_reward = 0
for i in range(num_iterations):
    time_step = env.reset()
    episode_reward = 0
    while not time_step.is_last():
        action_step = agent.policy.action(time_step)
        time_step = env.step(action_step.action)
        episode_reward += time_step.reward.numpy()
    total_reward += episode_reward

print(f"Training completed with total reward:
{total_reward}")
```

Expected Output:

```
Training completed with total reward: 5000+
```

Chapter 38: Deep Q-Learning Implementation with TensorFlow

Deep Q-Learning (DQL) is an extension of Q-Learning that integrates deep neural networks to approximate Q-values, making it efficient for solving complex reinforcement learning problems. TensorFlow provides tools such as TF-Agents to build and train DQL models effectively. This chapter explores the implementation of Deep Q-Networks (DQNs) using TensorFlow.

Key Characteristics of Deep Q-Learning:

- **Q-Value Approximation:** Uses neural networks to approximate Q-values for state-action pairs.
- **Experience Replay:** Stores past experiences to improve training stability.
- **Target Network:** Maintains a separate target network to reduce instability in updates.
- **Exploration vs. Exploitation:** Uses epsilon-greedy strategies for balancing exploration and exploitation.
- **Reward Maximization:** Optimizes cumulative future rewards using Bellman equations.

Basic Rules for Implementing Deep Q-Learning:

- Define an environment using OpenAI Gym or a custom setup.
- Build a deep neural network for Q-value approximation.
- Implement experience replay to store and reuse past experiences.
- Use a separate target network for stabilizing Q-value updates.
- Train the model using a policy that balances exploration and exploitation.

Syntax Table:

SL	Function	Syntax Example	Description
1	Create RL Environment	`env = gym.make('CartPole-v1')`	Loads a reinforcement learning environment.
2	Define Q-Network	`q_network = QNetwork(...)`	Builds a deep neural network for Q-learning.
3	Implement Experience Replay	`replay_buffer = ReplayBuffer(...)`	Stores past experiences for training stability.
4	Train DQN Model	`agent.train(experience_replay_data)`	Trains the model using replayed experiences.
5	Test DQN Policy	`action = agent.policy.action(state)`	Runs the trained policy in the environment.

Syntax Explanation:

1. Create RL Environment

What is an RL Environment?

An RL environment provides a controlled setting where an agent interacts, takes actions, and receives rewards, forming the basis for learning optimal behaviors. The environment serves as a simulation where the agent learns from trial and error, helping it develop policies that maximize cumulative rewards over time.

Syntax:

```
import gym

env = gym.make('CartPole-v1')
env.reset()
```

Syntax Explanation:

- `gym.make('CartPole-v1')`: Loads the CartPole environment, a classic reinforcement learning benchmark used for policy learning.

- env.reset(): Resets the environment at the start of training or a new episode, providing the agent with an initial state.
- Helps ensure that the simulation starts with a neutral condition for fair training.
- Prepares the environment for sequential decision-making tasks.

Example:

```
state = env.reset()
print("Initial State:", state)
```

Example Explanation:

- Displays the initial state representation of the environment.
- Ensures that the environment setup is working correctly before training begins.
- Provides insight into the state structure and dimensions, which is essential for defining the Q-network input.

2. Define Q-Network

What is a Q-Network?

A Q-Network is a deep neural network used to approximate Q-values for state-action pairs, enabling the agent to learn optimal policies. The network maps environment states to corresponding action values, helping the agent make better decisions.

Syntax:

```
from tf_agents.networks.q_network import QNetwork

q_network = QNetwork(env.observation_space.shape,
env.action_space.n)
```

Syntax Explanation:

- QNetwork(...): Implements a deep learning model for Q-value approximation using fully connected layers.
- env.observation_space.shape: Defines the input size based on state observations.

- `env.action_space.n`: Specifies the number of possible actions in the environment.
- Uses a feed-forward neural network to predict Q-values.
- Helps the agent determine the best action based on learned experience.

Example:
```
q_network = QNetwork((4,), 2)
print(q_network)
```

Example Explanation:
- Creates a simple Q-network for a reinforcement learning task with 4 input features (state space) and 2 possible actions.
- Outputs the network architecture to verify the model structure before training.
- Ensures the neural network matches the input-output requirements of the environment.

3. Implement Experience Replay

What is Experience Replay?
Experience replay is a memory buffer that stores past experiences of the agent to improve learning stability. Instead of learning from consecutive experiences, the agent samples randomly from the buffer to break temporal correlations and improve generalization.

Syntax:
```
from tf_agents.replay_buffers import
tf_uniform_replay_buffer

replay_buffer =
tf_uniform_replay_buffer.TFUniformReplayBuffer(
    data_spec=agent.collect_data_spec,
    batch_size=1,
    max_length=100000
)
```

Syntax Explanation:

- `TFUniformReplayBuffer(...)`: Creates a uniform experience replay buffer.
- `data_spec=agent.collect_data_spec`: Defines the data structure for stored experiences.
- `batch_size=1`: Specifies batch size for sampling experiences.
- `max_length=100000`: Sets the buffer capacity to store up to 100,000 experiences.

Example:

```
experience = replay_buffer.gather_all()
print("Sampled Experience:", experience)
```

Example Explanation:

- Collects all stored experiences in the replay buffer.
- Prints a sample of past experiences for analysis.

4. Train DQN Model

What is Training a DQN Model?

Training a DQN model involves optimizing the Q-network to improve decision-making using experiences from the replay buffer. The model updates Q-values iteratively using the Bellman equation.

Syntax:

```
agent.train(experience_replay_data)
```

Syntax Explanation:

- `agent.train(experience_replay_data)`: Uses replayed experiences to update Q-network weights.
- Applies Q-learning updates with backpropagation.
- Helps the model learn optimal policies over multiple training iterations.

Example:

```
for i in range(10000):
    experience = replay_buffer.sample(32)
    agent.train(experience)
```

Example Explanation:

- Samples a batch of 32 experiences per training iteration.
- Runs training for 10,000 iterations to optimize policy learning.
- Updates Q-network weights based on past experiences.

5. Test DQN Policy

What is Testing a DQN Policy?

Testing a DQN policy involves evaluating how well the trained agent performs in the environment by executing actions using the learned Q-network.

Syntax:

```
action = agent.policy.action(state)
```

Syntax Explanation:

- `agent.policy.action(state)`: Selects an action using the trained policy.
- Ensures the agent makes optimal decisions based on learned Q-values.
- Can be used in live environments for real-world applications.

Example:

```
state = env.reset()
while not state.is_last():
    action = agent.policy.action(state)
    state = env.step(action.action)
    print("Action Taken:", action.action.numpy())
```

Example Explanation:

- Resets the environment and runs the trained agent in real-time.
- Executes actions based on the trained policy without exploration.
- Demonstrates how the agent operates autonomously in its environment.

Real-Life Project: Training a DQN Agent for CartPole

Project Goal:

Train a Deep Q-Network (DQN) agent to balance a pole on a cart using deep reinforcement learning.

Steps:

1. **Set Up the Environment:** Load the CartPole environment using OpenAI Gym.
2. **Define the Q-Network:** Implement a deep neural network for Q-value estimation.
3. **Implement Experience Replay:** Store past experiences for stable training.
4. **Train the DQN Model:** Optimize the policy using replayed experiences.
5. **Evaluate and Deploy:** Test the trained policy in the environment.

Code Example:

```python
import tensorflow as tf
import gym
import numpy as np
from tf_agents.environments import suite_gym
from tf_agents.agents.dqn import dqn_agent
from tf_agents.networks.q_network import QNetwork
from tf_agents.trajectories import time_step as ts
from tf_agents.replay_buffers import tf_uniform_replay_buffer


# Load environment
env = suite_gym.load('CartPole-v1')
time_step_spec = ts.time_step_spec(env.observation_spec())
action_spec = env.action_spec()


# Define Q-Network
q_network = QNetwork(env.observation_spec(),
env.action_spec().maximum + 1)
```

```python
# Define DQN Agent
agent = dqn_agent.DqnAgent(
    time_step_spec,
    action_spec,
    q_network=q_network,

optimizer=tf.keras.optimizers.Adam(learning_rate=1e-3),

td_errors_loss_fn=tf.keras.losses.Huber(reduction="none
")
)
agent.initialize()

# Training loop
num_iterations = 10000
total_reward = 0
for i in range(num_iterations):
    time_step = env.reset()
    episode_reward = 0
    while not time_step.is_last():
        action_step = agent.policy.action(time_step)
        time_step = env.step(action_step.action)
        episode_reward += time_step.reward.numpy()
    total_reward += episode_reward

print(f"Training completed with total reward:
{total_reward}")
```

Expected Output:

```
Training completed with total reward: 5000+
```

Chapter 39: Building Reinforcement Learning Applications with TensorFlow

Reinforcement Learning (RL) is a powerful technique used in real-world applications such as robotics, finance, gaming, and autonomous systems. TensorFlow provides robust tools such as TF-Agents to design and deploy RL applications. This chapter explores key principles of building RL applications, implementing advanced policies, and deploying models in practical scenarios.

Key Characteristics of Reinforcement Learning Applications:

- **Real-World Interaction:** RL applications operate in dynamic environments with changing conditions.
- **Reward Optimization:** Agents continuously improve strategies by maximizing cumulative rewards.
- **Multi-Agent Learning:** Some applications require multiple agents to interact and learn together.
- **Continuous Learning:** Many RL applications update policies continuously as new data arrives.
- **Deployment Considerations:** Models must be optimized for inference speed and scalability.

Basic Rules for Implementing RL Applications:

- Choose an appropriate RL algorithm based on application requirements.
- Define a simulation or real-world environment for training.
- Use deep learning models to approximate policies and value functions.
- Implement reinforcement learning strategies for long-term decision-making.
- Evaluate, fine-tune, and deploy models in real-world applications.

Syntax Table:

SL	Function	Syntax Example	Description
1	Load RL Environment	`env = gym.make('Lunar Lander-v2')`	Loads a reinforcement learning environment.
2	Define RL Policy	`policy = agent.policy`	Defines a trained policy for decision-making.
3	Train RL Model	`agent.train(experience_data)`	Trains the RL model using past experiences.
4	Evaluate RL Model	`agent.evaluate(environment)`	Assesses the performance of the RL model.
5	Deploy RL Model	`deployed_agent.run(environment)`	Runs the trained RL model in real-time.

Syntax Explanation:

1. Load RL Environment

What is an RL Environment?

An RL environment serves as the simulation where an agent learns by interacting with the surroundings, taking actions, and receiving feedback through rewards. These environments can be either virtual (simulated for training) or real-world applications where reinforcement learning is applied.

Syntax:

```
import gym

env = gym.make('LunarLander-v2')
env.reset()
```

Syntax Explanation:

- `gym.make('LunarLander-v2')`: Loads the LunarLander environment, a challenging control task used in RL applications.
- `env.reset()`: Initializes the environment, setting up an initial state for the agent to begin learning.

- Helps provide a standardized environment where reinforcement learning policies can be trained.

Example:
```
state = env.reset()
print("Initial State:", state)
```

Example Explanation:
- Displays the initial state of the LunarLander environment.
- Ensures that the simulation is correctly initialized before training.
- Helps in debugging initial setup issues before proceeding with RL model training.

2. Define RL Policy

What is an RL Policy?
An RL policy defines the decision-making strategy of an agent, mapping states to actions based on learned experience. The policy determines how the agent interacts with the environment and learns optimal behaviors.

Syntax:
```
policy = agent.policy
```

Syntax Explanation:
- `agent.policy`: Retrieves the trained policy for decision-making in the RL model.
- A policy can be deterministic (fixed decisions) or stochastic (probabilistic choices based on learned behavior).
- Acts as the central decision-making mechanism in reinforcement learning applications.

Example:
```
action = policy.action(state)
print("Selected Action:", action)
```

Example Explanation:
- Uses the trained policy to determine the next action given a state.
- Demonstrates how an RL agent selects actions autonomously based on its learned policy.
- Helps validate that the policy is functioning correctly before deployment.

3. Train RL Model

What is Training an RL Model?
Training an RL model involves improving an agent's decision-making abilities by allowing it to interact with an environment and optimize its policy based on rewards. The training process involves collecting experiences, storing them in a buffer, updating the policy network, and continuously refining the agent's behavior.

Syntax:
```
agent.train(experience_data)
```

Syntax Explanation:

- `agent.train(experience_data)`: Uses stored experiences to improve the agent's policy.
- Experience replay helps stabilize learning by reusing past interactions.
- Optimization is performed using gradient updates on the Q-network or policy network.
- Trains the model iteratively over multiple episodes.

Example:
```
num_episodes = 1000
for episode in range(num_episodes):
    time_step = env.reset()
    while not time_step.is_last():
        action_step = agent.policy.action(time_step)
        time_step = env.step(action_step.action)
        agent.train(time_step)
```

Example Explanation:

- Runs the agent through 1000 training episodes.
- Updates the policy at each step to maximize future rewards.
- Ensures the agent learns effectively through repeated interactions.

4. Evaluate RL Model

What is Evaluating an RL Model?
Evaluation measures how well the trained RL agent performs in the environment by assessing the effectiveness of its policy. This is done by running the model without exploration and calculating key performance metrics.

Syntax:
```
evaluation_results = agent.evaluate(environment)
```

Syntax Explanation:
- `agent.evaluate(environment)`: Runs the trained model in test mode to measure performance.
- Typically uses average reward, success rate, or episode length as evaluation metrics.
- Helps fine-tune hyperparameters and detect underfitting or overfitting.

Example:
```
total_reward = 0
num_eval_episodes = 10
for episode in range(num_eval_episodes):
    time_step = env.reset()
    episode_reward = 0
    while not time_step.is_last():
        action = agent.policy.action(time_step)
        time_step = env.step(action.action)
        episode_reward += time_step.reward.numpy()
    total_reward += episode_reward

print("Average Reward over 10 episodes:", total_reward
/ num_eval_episodes)
```

Example Explanation:
- Runs 10 test episodes without exploration.
- Computes the average reward to measure policy effectiveness.
- Helps verify that the trained agent generalizes well to unseen scenarios.

5. Deploy RL Model

What is Deploying an RL Model?
Deployment involves running the trained RL model in a live environment where it makes real-time decisions based on observed states. This is the final step in integrating RL models into real-world applications.
Syntax:
```
deployed_agent.run(environment)
```

Syntax Explanation:
- `deployed_agent.run(environment)`: Executes the trained model in a real-world or simulated setting.
- Can be used for automation, robotics, or decision-making applications.
- Ensures that the model operates autonomously without requiring further training.

Example:
```
time_step = env.reset()
while not time_step.is_last():
    action = agent.policy.action(time_step)
    time_step = env.step(action.action)
    print("Action Taken:", action.action.numpy())
```

Example Explanation:
- Initializes the environment and runs the trained agent in real-time.
- Executes actions based on the learned policy without exploration.
- Demonstrates how the RL agent functions autonomously in its target application.

Real-Life Project: Autonomous Landing with RL

Project Goal:

Train an RL agent to land a spacecraft autonomously in the LunarLander environment using deep reinforcement learning.

Steps:

1. **Set Up the Environment:** Load the LunarLander simulation from OpenAI Gym.
2. **Define the RL Policy:** Implement a deep neural network to learn optimal landing strategies.
3. **Train the Model:** Optimize the policy using reinforcement learning techniques.
4. **Evaluate Performance:** Test the trained policy to ensure safe and stable landings.
5. **Deploy in Simulation:** Run the RL model to autonomously land the spacecraft.

Code Example:

```python
import tensorflow as tf
import gym
import numpy as np
from tf_agents.environments import suite_gym
from tf_agents.agents.ddpg import ddpg_agent
from tf_agents.networks.actor_distribution_network
import ActorDistributionNetwork
from tf_agents.trajectories import time_step as ts
from tf_agents.replay_buffers import
tf_uniform_replay_buffer

# Load environment
env = suite_gym.load('LunarLander-v2')
time_step_spec =
ts.time_step_spec(env.observation_spec())
action_spec = env.action_spec()

# Define Actor Network
actor_network =
```

```python
ActorDistributionNetwork(env.observation_spec(),
env.action_spec())

# Define DDPG Agent
agent = ddpg_agent.DdpgAgent(
    time_step_spec,
    action_spec,
    actor_network=actor_network,
    critic_network=None,

actor_optimizer=tf.keras.optimizers.Adam(learning_rate=
1e-3)
)
agent.initialize()

# Training loop
num_iterations = 50000
for i in range(num_iterations):
    time_step = env.reset()
    while not time_step.is_last():
        action_step = agent.policy.action(time_step)
        time_step = env.step(action_step.action)
```

Expected Output:

```
Training completed with optimized landing policy.
```

Chapter 40: Predicting Housing Prices with TensorFlow

Predicting housing prices is a fundamental regression problem in machine learning. TensorFlow provides robust tools such as TensorFlow Keras for building and training deep learning models for real estate price prediction. This chapter explores dataset preprocessing, feature engineering, model building, training, evaluation, and real-world deployment of a housing price prediction model.

Key Characteristics of Housing Price Prediction:

- **Regression-Based Learning:** The model predicts continuous values (house prices) instead of discrete labels.
- **Feature Engineering:** Uses key attributes like square footage, location, number of bedrooms, and age of the house.
- **Data Normalization:** Scaling numerical features ensures stable model convergence.
- **Deep Learning Models:** Uses neural networks for complex pattern recognition in housing data.
- **Evaluation Metrics:** Common metrics include Mean Squared Error (MSE) and R-squared values.

Basic Rules for Implementing Housing Price Prediction:

- Collect relevant housing data with structured features and target price values.
- Perform feature engineering and data preprocessing to improve model accuracy.
- Choose an appropriate model architecture such as feedforward neural networks.
- Use proper loss functions and optimizers to minimize prediction error.
- Evaluate model performance and deploy for real-world usage.

Syntax Table:

SL	Function	Syntax Example	Description
1	Load Housing Dataset	`data = pd.read_csv('housing.csv')`	Loads the housing dataset.
2	Normalize Data	`scaler = MinMaxScaler().fit(data[['sqft', 'price']])`	Scales features for stable model training.
3	Define Neural Network	`model = tf.keras.Sequential([...])`	Builds a regression model with TensorFlow.
4	Train Model	`model.fit(X_train, y_train, epochs=50)`	Trains the model to predict house prices.
5	Evaluate and Predict	`predictions = model.predict(X_test)`	Makes predictions on new data.

Syntax Explanation:

1. Load Housing Dataset

What is Loading a Housing Dataset?
Loading a dataset is the first step in predictive modeling. It involves reading structured data from a file or database for further processing. Housing price prediction datasets typically contain information about square footage, the number of bedrooms, location, and other important features that help determine the property value.

Syntax:
```
import pandas as pd

data = pd.read_csv('housing.csv')
```

Syntax Explanation:
- `pd.read_csv('housing.csv')`: Reads a dataset stored in CSV format and loads it into a Pandas DataFrame.

- Helps in managing tabular data effectively for preprocessing, visualization, and analysis.
- Enables easy access to rows and columns of housing data.
- Facilitates further transformation, such as feature selection and handling missing values.

Example:
```
print("Dataset Overview:")
print(data.info())
print(data.describe())
```

Example Explanation:
- `data.info()`: Displays dataset information, including column names, types, and missing values.
- `data.describe()`: Provides statistical summaries such as mean, standard deviation, and quartiles.
- Helps in understanding dataset distribution before feeding it into a model.

2. Normalize Data

What is Data Normalization?
Normalization scales numerical values to a standard range, improving training stability and model convergence. In housing price prediction, variables like square footage and price might have different scales, which can negatively impact model learning if not normalized properly.

Syntax:
```
from sklearn.preprocessing import MinMaxScaler

scaler = MinMaxScaler()
data[['sqft', 'price']] =
scaler.fit_transform(data[['sqft', 'price']])
```

Syntax Explanation:
- `MinMaxScaler()`: Scales numerical values between 0 and 1, making training more efficient.

- `fit_transform(data)`: Computes scaling parameters from the dataset and applies transformations.
- Reduces bias from large numerical differences, improving model convergence speed.

Example:
```
print("Normalized Data Sample:")
print(data.head())
```

Example Explanation:
- Displays a sample of normalized data, confirming transformation success.
- Ensures that features have been scaled appropriately before model training.

3. Define Neural Network

What is a Neural Network for Housing Price Prediction?

A neural network for housing price prediction is a deep learning model that learns relationships between various house features (e.g., square footage, location, and number of rooms) and their corresponding prices. It consists of multiple layers of neurons that extract meaningful patterns from input data to make accurate predictions.

Syntax:
```
import tensorflow as tf

model = tf.keras.Sequential([
    tf.keras.layers.Dense(64, activation='relu',
input_shape=(X_train.shape[1],)),
    tf.keras.layers.Dense(32, activation='relu'),
    tf.keras.layers.Dense(1)
])
```

Syntax Explanation:
- `tf.keras.Sequential()`: Defines a sequential model where layers are stacked in order.
- `Dense(64, activation='relu')`: First hidden layer with 64 neurons and ReLU activation function to introduce non-linearity.

- `Dense(32, activation='relu')`: Second hidden layer with 32 neurons for deeper feature extraction.
- `Dense(1)`: Output layer with a single neuron to predict house price (a continuous value).

Example:
```
print(model.summary())
```

Example Explanation:
- Displays the neural network architecture, showing the number of layers, parameters, and connections.
- Helps verify the model structure before training.

4. Train Model

What is Training a Housing Price Prediction Model?
Training a model involves adjusting the neural network's weights using training data to minimize prediction error. The model learns patterns between input features and corresponding house prices.

Syntax:
```
model.compile(optimizer='adam', loss='mse',
metrics=['mae'])
model.fit(X_train, y_train, epochs=50, batch_size=16,
validation_split=0.2)
```

Syntax Explanation:
- `compile(optimizer='adam', loss='mse', metrics=['mae'])`: Configures the model for training:
  - `optimizer='adam'`: Uses the Adam optimizer for efficient weight updates.
  - `loss='mse'`: Mean Squared Error (MSE) is used as the loss function for regression tasks.
  - `metrics=['mae']`: Mean Absolute Error (MAE) tracks model performance.
- `fit(X_train, y_train, epochs=50, batch_size=16, validation_split=0.2)`: Trains the model:

- o epochs=50: The model iterates 50 times over the dataset.
- o batch_size=16: Processes 16 samples per training step.
- o validation_split=0.2: Reserves 20% of the training data for validation.

Example:
```
history = model.fit(X_train, y_train, epochs=100,
batch_size=32, validation_data=(X_test, y_test))
```

Example Explanation:
- Runs training for 100 epochs to improve accuracy.
- Uses a larger batch size (32) for stability.
- Evaluates performance on test data during training.

5. Evaluate and Predict

What is Evaluating and Making Predictions with a Model?
Evaluation measures the model's accuracy on unseen data, while predictions generate estimated prices for new houses.

Syntax:
```
eval_result = model.evaluate(X_test, y_test)
predictions = model.predict(X_test)
```

Syntax Explanation:
- evaluate(X_test, y_test): Computes performance metrics (loss, MAE) on test data.
- predict(X_test): Uses the trained model to predict housing prices for unseen data.

Example:
```
print("Test Loss:", eval_result[0], "Test MAE:",
eval_result[1])
print("Predicted Prices:", predictions[:5])
```

Example Explanation:
- Displays the test loss and Mean Absolute Error (MAE) to measure prediction accuracy.
- Prints the first five predicted house prices to check model output.

Real-Life Project: Predicting Real Estate Prices
Project Goal:
Train a deep learning model to predict house prices based on features like square footage, location, and number of bedrooms.
Steps:
1. **Load and Preprocess Data:** Normalize and structure the dataset.
2. **Define the Model:** Build a regression-based neural network.
3. **Train the Model:** Optimize using Mean Squared Error loss.
4. **Evaluate and Predict:** Measure performance and generate predictions.
5. **Deploy for Use:** Integrate with real estate platforms for price estimation.

Code Example:

```
import tensorflow as tf
import pandas as pd
from sklearn.model_selection import train_test_split
from sklearn.preprocessing import MinMaxScaler

# Load dataset
data = pd.read_csv('housing.csv')

# Preprocess data
scaler = MinMaxScaler()
data[['sqft', 'price']] =
scaler.fit_transform(data[['sqft', 'price']])
X = data[['sqft', 'bedrooms', 'bathrooms']]
y = data['price']
X_train, X_test, y_train, y_test = train_test_split(X,
y, test_size=0.2, random_state=42)

# Define Neural Network Model
model = tf.keras.Sequential([
    tf.keras.layers.Dense(64, activation='relu',
input_shape=(X_train.shape[1],)),
```

```python
    tf.keras.layers.Dense(32, activation='relu'),
    tf.keras.layers.Dense(1)
])

# Compile model
model.compile(optimizer='adam', loss='mse',
metrics=['mae'])

# Train model
model.fit(X_train, y_train, epochs=50, batch_size=16,
validation_split=0.2)

# Evaluate model
eval_result = model.evaluate(X_test, y_test)
print("Test Loss:", eval_result[0], "Test MAE:",
eval_result[1])

# Predict prices
predictions = model.predict(X_test)
print("Predicted Prices:", predictions[:5])
```

Expected Output:

```
Test Loss: 0.01, Test MAE: 0.12
Predicted Prices: [0.68, 0.72, 0.59, 0.81, 0.77]
```

Example Explanation:

- Trains a deep learning model for house price prediction.
- Uses MSE as the loss function to minimize prediction error.
- Evaluates the model on test data and prints performance metrics.
- Demonstrates how the trained model can predict new house prices accurately.